PROPHETIC TIMELINE For NATIONS REVIVAL

Unveiling Divine Oracles and Strategy for Effective Intercession

ATRIA STEPHEN

© 2017 by Stephen Atria
First Published in 2017

All rights reserved.
No part of this publication may be reproduced, stored in a retrieval system, or transmitted in any form or by any means, electronic, mechanical, photocopying, recording or otherwise, without prior written permission of the author.

Printing and/or ordering information
Stephen Atria
atriabiz@gmail.com
+256782963815/+256750490098

Cover Photo by
Cover Design by RENSA PRINTERS LTD +256 782 822 714
Printed and bound in the Uganda

First edition

ISBN: 978-9970-9699-0-6

Dedication

I dedicate this piece of work to my beloved saviour Jesus Christ for loving me to death. To my lovely wife Akikoli Scovia for taking care, praying and for her companionship.

Acknowledgement

I wish to sincerely appreciate my mentors Rutaisire Augustine and Sewanyana Fred who saw the gift of God in me and nurtured me in the ministry to become effective minister and servant of God.

I wish to thank Liberty World Outreach ministries Arua for the support, care, prayer and being around me. You are the champions around me and reason my calling is growing and becoming meaningful.

I acknowledge my friends in Agape Christian fellowship Pastor Patrick Jacamunga, Pastor Sam Feta, Gilman Izuma and his wife Fabiola, John and Queen Adriko, Emmanuel Candia, Xavier and Sany and all others for the prophecies, opportunity to minister and share Kingdom grace.
Thank you my publisher Sam for the wonderful work.

Introduction

All over the world, there is an intensifying decay in morals as darkness gets dark and evil finds its way onto our moral dining table to change the diet of our morals. Some people and churches are experiencing dryness and emptiness as legislations and rights movements try to shut the mouth and prophetic voice of the church. The overarching question we ask is what do we do and what will happen next?

In reality however we are living in the most exciting time in history and God is upto something big. Technology makes it possible to preach the Gospel to impenetrable regions and there seems to be great spiritual hunger as well in many parts of the world. The darkness we see is not the problem but light is the problem. When light shines, it dispels any darkness regardless of how dark it is and we are to let our light shine before the world and let them see our good works.

There is a wind of revival and awakening blowing in the nations as prophetic timelines for nation's revival is at hand. This book comes to unzip and unveil prophetic seasons and timelines for the epicentre of the great awakening the world is yet to see in all history of mankind.

Whenever God speaks, it is not for observation or to occupy discussion forums but for obedience, declaration and manifestation. We are all accountable to respond to this great cause. This book will bring you face to face with prophecies and divine oracles for regions and nations and also face to face with God who is revealing Himself and plans. More so you will have grips with strategy to birth destinies of nations. Get ready for this journey of encounter of a lifetime for His glory. Amen.

Stephen Atria
Liberty To the Captives International
 atriabiz@gmail.com
+256782963815/+256750490098
July 2017

PROPHETIC TIMELINE FOR NATIONS REVIVAL

CONTENTS

CHAPTER ONE
100 Year Revival Prophesy Timeline For The World

Maria Woodworth Etter prophesy
The renowned evangelist Maria Woodworth Etter began a revival on July 2, 1913 at Stone Church.   As Christians prayed around the altar one evening, Sister Woodworth-Etter and others gave the following powerful prophecy and divine promise, which they prophesied would occur within 100 years of the 1913 Chicago Visitation. She prophesied of this coming End Time Revival...."We are not yet up to the fullness of the Former Rain and that when the Latter Rain comes, it will far exceed anything we have seen!"

William Seymour prophesy
William Seymour, the leader of the Azusa Street Awakening, also prophesied that in 100 years there would be an outpouring of God's Spirit and His Shekinah Glory that would be greater and more far reaching than what was experienced at Azusa.

It has been almost 100 years since these prophecies were given... we have reached the time of the fulfilment of these 100 year old prophecies. We must be diligent to pray, intercede and protect what the Lord is doing. We must encourage and edify one another as never before. We must crucify every critical, judgmental and religious spirit that may be within us

GOD'S HEART FOR NATIONS

1. Jehovah Jireh – God cares for His creation and directs the affairs of nations (Ps 65:9)
2. All nations will be blessed. Genesis 12 :1-3 talks about the seed of Abraham Jesus the Messiah (blessing of eternal life)
3. The day of the Lord is for all or will affect all nations (Obadiah 15, Jeremiah 25:29 cf 30, Amos 4:7, Hosea 11:8-9
4. All nations are recipients of Gods mercy. Exodus 33:19, Jer 18:7-10, Jonah
5. Nations benefit from Israel's blessing and as worshippers of God. Psalms 47, 67, zech 8:11-13
6. Every nation is blessed with Gods salvation. Isaiah 19:23-25
7. Every nation has identity. Psalms 87, Amos 9:11-12
8. All nations history is under Gods control because God is universal and concerned with the history of all people not just Israel.

THE MISSION OF GOD TO ALL NATIONS

1. The nation in creation and providence includes all people and governments
2. The nations are not outside of Biblical record but they appear right after the flood, they are always present either in foreground or background in the story
3. The final picture of nations is shown in the book of Revelations 21:24-27
4. Nations are part of the created and redeemed humanity or people groups

5. All nations stand under God's judgment. For example in the book of Exodus God judged not only Pharaoh but all Egypt.

6. Any nation can be an agent of judgment God uses to judge another nation. For example Israel was used to judge the Canaanites and other nations like the Amalekites, Midianites, Arabs, Arameans, Assyrians, Babylonians all served in turn in this way.

CHAPTER TWO

Prophetic Transition For West Nile
24/09/2015

THE EPICENTRE

In my vision, the map of Africa was brought before me vibrating and fire filled it and then the nation of Uganda appeared distinct brightened and filled with fire. Then West Nile region appeared on the map filled with fire as the Epicentre.

THREE REVIVAL PATHS THROUGH AFRICA

This glorious light and fire emanating from West Nile and moved through Africa, Asia, Europe and America in three paths as follows

1. The first one took the northern path through South Sudan, Sudan, Egypt and when it reached Egypt the fire spread there because there was a fountain head there and from Egypt it split into two, one went to Asia towards India where there is a fountain head and the other one to Europe heading to Netherlands and spread all over Europe.

2. The second path of light took the path through south via Lake Victoria, Tanzania and in it Tanzania it spread around Dodoma, then went through Zambia to Namibia where

it spread within southern Africa. From Namibia the fire went across Atlantic Ocean to America continent pointing to California where there is a fountain head and it spread throughout America.

3. The third path of the fire took the way through Congo, central Africa where there is another fountain head and spread in that part of Africa. From Central Africa it split into three, one going to Nigeria a fountain head spreading fire around, another to Ghana another fountain head and the other to Senegal another fountain head.

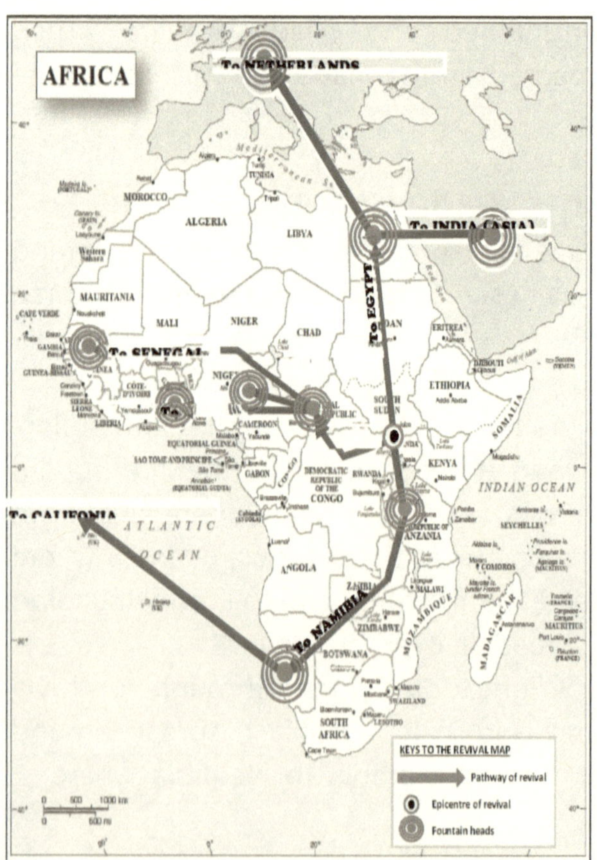

INTERPRETATION

1. The light represents revival and renewal that will sweep through these nations and bring awakening to the world.
2. West Nile is my fountain head and epicentre from which revival will spring and that I will use these last days to water my garden
3. West Nile is my gateway to the nations and I have been training my sons and daughters in west Nile for this purpose.
4. I will send you as my apostles and missionaries to the nations to take the fire of revival and disciple nations. West Nile should prepare to fund and support missionaries carrying the revival on these 3 highways of revival
5. The revival will flow with healing and refreshing for the nations and for my people who are languishing in pain. They will drink from my waters of salvation and be refreshed
6. I made you to look like ignorant and backward people who are difficult to deal with because I was preserving you so that you would not be defiled. I caused you to be ignored so that you may turn to me and learn my ways.
7. The year 2016 is a year of harvest and will open the door for economic deliverance and economic revival in the land.
8. West Nile will send and sponsor missionaries on these 3 highways of revival. They will sponsor ministries of chosen vessels sent on revival mission
9. West Nile people are my warriors for demolishing strongholds and bringing freedom to nations. A fearless people but sincere in their heart, fathers to generations and my weapon for yoke breaking.

WEST NILE'S TIMING AND EXCUSES

1. The spirit of the Lord came upon me on 31/05/2017
    1. 11:15pm in such a mighty power to the point I was scared in the vision and I knelt and said "God if you are looking for someone to use, here I am" and immediately the Lord Jesus appeared in a vision with great glory that God's presence penetrated my bones even when I came out of the vision it was so strong that I kept crying.
    2. Thus says the Lord; Time has come for me to shake the land, to restore those who are faithful and watching. Time has come for me to release my people.
    3. Thus says the Lord, I have waited too long and heard voices rise to me, time has come for me to walk through the land of West Nile. I will overturn the gods, to judge wickedness, to overturn ungodliness and my enemies. I will trample under feet everything that offends my holiness.
    4. I have come personally to open my fountains, the unclean will not fetch from it, the compromising shall not, only clean vessels will fetch from it. Days of taking my word for granted have passed and I arise like a warrior for the burden of those who have been misrepresenting me.
    5. The nations are in pain and the people are perishing yet my servant West Nile is full of excuses. How long will you have excuses? My hand is upon you, wake up, and wake up for I will show wonders, restore hope.
    6. I will build the broken walls in the nations whose walls, gates are broken and are in reproach, wilderness and pain but for my servant West Nile the labour pains have started but there is no strength to give birth. I will walk in the land

7. to give strength, to empower and raise up people.

8. Why take your call as a small thing but concentrate on building your personal and denominational empires? My heart yearns for the souls in the nations that do not know me and yet are searching and seeking for me. My heart yearns for children who are innocently being corrupted and misled to idols.

9. My servant is intimidated by witches, circumstances, opinion of others and what you see. If you do not arise, my hand will be heavy on you. It will be better for Jonah in the belly of the fish than for you if you rebel against me. It will be better for Israel in the wilderness than for you.

10. My servant, hear my words again; beginning this year

11. 2017, I will start walking in this land, raising up an army and a people that will follow in my ways whom I will send to carry my name, power, salvation and grace to the nations. A renewal, revival and restoration will run through the nations for 40 years from 2017 to 2057 and I will sustain my garden, magnify my name and my fame will reach nations that did not know me. I will bring in those that were not in my sheepfold before that great and terrible day.

10. I will send my sons as chosen messengers, therefore amend your ways, cleanse your vessels, turn away from wickedness and be separate. I call you to the place of consecration, repent and turn to me, wake up you who are asleep, arise you complacent one and my glory will shine on you. I have made you my delight and chosen vessels.

11. Give no more excuses for the time for me to walk in the land is at hand. I will make a difference between those

12. who fear me and those who profane my name by their shameless actions and behaviours. Those who call on me from a pure heart, I will make them glad and nothing will make them afraid because I will lead them gently like a shepherd carrying a lamb says the Lord.

INSTRUCTIONS

1. Establish altars in west Nile to intensify the spiritual climate. Your lives should be dedicated altars to me (Romans 12:1-2)
2. Declare prayer and fasting for the pillars of revival comprising of all intercessors of west Nile. Pillars are spiritual territorial commanders for nations.
3. Establish a prayer retreat centre called "GATEWAY OF NATIONS". In this place I will birth revival fire and refresh my people.
4. Let my people have a praise offering every month to activate the season's flow

CHAPTER THREE

Revival Prophecy for Uganda

A PROPHESY GIVEN ON 2ND JUNE 2003

Note: this prophesy was given to me and I was commanded to close the book and not speak it forth until the day I will be instructed to speak forth. In January 2016 the ban was lifted and I was told to speak forth the prophesy to the nation as follows;

SPIRITUAL FOUNTAIN FOR NATIONS

My servant Uganda, I called you before the foundations of the earth. I called you to sustain my people, to proclaim liberty among the gentile nations and to disciple my people.

Indeed you are a pearl to me. Your water the Nile sustained and refreshed my servants Abraham in Egypt when he fled the famine, Jacob and his seed for 430 years during their abode and slavery in Egypt. Israel drank from your waters and was refreshed and sustained until I brought them to the land I promised their father Abraham, Isaac and Jacob.

When King Herod wanted to kill my son Jesus Christ, I sent Him to Egypt, a nation whose land your waters sustain and He drank also from the Nile waters. In these days I have remembered my mercies unto you and I have purposed to do good to you. In the same way your physical water the Nile sustained and refreshed Israel and my son Jesus in Egypt so your spiritual waters are to water the nations and refresh them with revival that the nations may find liberty and be healed. Nations are coming to drink again from your spiritual waters.

Behold I kindle a fire of liberty in you, that you may go and proclaim liberty to the nations and you shall speak to the princes of darkness, "thus says the Lord, let my people go free that they may worship me". The rulers of this Dark Age will surely resist you but my glory shall arise from the east and my standard shall be lifted against him.
Arise gird up your strength my servant, be complacent no more, and let your birth pangs be manifested.

"Let them give glory to the LORD, and declare his praise in the coastlands. The LORD goes out like a mighty man, like a man of war he stirs up his zeal; he cries out, he shouts aloud, he shows himself mighty against his foes. For a long time I have held my peace; I have kept still and restrained myself; now I will cry out like a woman in labour; I will gasp and pant. I will lay waste mountains and hills, and dry up all their vegetation; I will turn the rivers into islands, and dry up the pools. And I will lead the blind in a way that they do not know, in paths that they have not known I will guide them. I will turn the darkness before them into light, the rough places into level ground. These are the things I do, and I do not forsake them.

They are turned back and utterly put to shame, who trust in carved idols, who say to metal images, "You are our gods." (Isaiah 42:12 – 17)

But my servant has taken my call a common thing. My servant listened but did not respond, my servant saw but did not act. Why is it that I called and you did not respond? He says: *"It is too light a thing that you should be my servant to raise up the tribes of Jacob and to bring back the preserved of Israel; I will make you as a light for the nations, that my salvation may reach to the end of the earth."* (Isaiah 49:6)

"Hear you deaf, and look, you blind, that you may see! Who is blind but my servant, or deaf as my messenger whom I send? Who is blind as my dedicated one, or blind as the servant of the LORD? He sees many things, but does not observe them; his ears are open, but he does not hear." Isaiah 42:18 - 20

Look in your ways and see why you are not prosperous and running a squeezed economy? You were a precious pearl in my sight but now you are faded like a garment. Why are you full of bloodshed, rebellion, hatred, envy and why does injustice reign in your house? You have been put on the scale and found wanting.

Look back to the rock you were cut from (go back to your call) and walk in my will and then you shall see my glory again in these days. I sent my messengers to you but their message you did not heed and considered it like a strange song.

Time is running out but I call again to you my servant that you may arise out of complacency.

Just like a merchant seeking a precious pearl went forth and sold all his belongings to buy the pearl so nations shall come and pour their wealth unto you. People great and small, old and young, will come to drink from your spiritual fountains as they seek for refreshment and restoration.

I am making you a model among the nations, in all your ways. Thus says the lord "copy no more from the nations because the rulers of this Dark Age has risen in some nations and caused abominations before my sight. I have cut them loose and given them up to their own ways and futility so that they will be ensnared by their own devices.

"For although they knew God, they did not honour him as God or give thanks to him, but they became futile in their thinking, and their foolish hearts were darkened. Claiming to be wise, they became fools, and exchanged the glory of the immortal God for images resembling mortal man and birds and animals and creeping things. Therefore God gave them up in the lusts of their hearts to impurity, to the dishonouring of their bodies among themselves, because they exchanged the truth about God for a lie and worshiped and served the creature rather than the Creator, who is blessed forever! Amen. For this reason God gave them up to dishonourable passions. For their women exchanged natural relations for those that are contrary to nature; and the men likewise gave up natural relations with women and were consumed with passion for one another, men committing shameless acts

with men and receiving in themselves the due penalty for their error. And since they did not see fit to acknowledge God, God gave them up to a debased mind to do what ought not to be done. They were filled with all manner of unrighteousness, evil, covetousness, malice. They are full of envy, murder, strife, deceit, maliciousness. They are gossips, slanderers, haters of God, insolent, haughty, boastful, inventors of evil, disobedient to parents, foolish, faithless, heartless, ruthless." (Romans1:21-31)

Travail oh my servant, travail for the nations and birth the knowledge and the fear of the Holy one in the nations. Awake to righteousness, gird up your strength and proclaim liberty to my people. Then shall your peace flow like a river, you will find favour, prosper in your entire goings and siblings shall stop pointing the finger and shedding of blood. Why is it that I called you and you did not consider? Is it because my hand is shortened to deliver the nations? If you regard not my call, then I will show you that my own right hand shall accomplish for me salvation for the nations. Hearken unto me and be stiff necked no more.

REVELATION OF UGANDA'S CALL IN THE NATIONAL ANTHEM

1. *Oh Uganda, may God uphold thee*
   we lay our future in thy hand. United
   free, for liberty,
   together we'll always stand

2. *Oh Uganda, the land of freedom*
   our love and labour we give
   and with neighbours all
   at our country's call
   in peace and friendship we'll live.

3. *Oh Uganda, the land that feeds us by*
   sun and fertile soil grown
   for our own dear land
   we'll always stand
   the pearl of Africa's crown

REVELATION

The first stanza or verse explains Uganda's call as follows.

- Uganda has found favour and her future has been upheld in the eyes of God.
- Uganda is to walk in unity before the Lord regardless of tribe and clans.
- Uganda is called to be a free nation and declare liberty (freedom) to nations in bondage.

The second stanza or verse explains Uganda's call as follows

- Uganda is called to carry the banners of freedom (spiritual and Physical)
- Develop love for our brothers in the nations by travailing and labouring in prayers
- Become responsible for peace of our neighbours by carrying the gospel of peace to the people of God, to sustain and refresh them.
- When you call peace to the neighbours, peace shall abide, for out of you shall flow streams of peace and friendship

The last verse or stanza explains the responsibility of every Ugandan to their nation

- Every Ugandan must stand and plead before God for sustenance of our economy, income sources and prosperity.
- We are to pray, love and work for the peace of Uganda
- Pray and cry to God to heal and bless the Pearl of Africa
- Because people neglected their own responsibility to their nation, Uganda remains defiled, wounded by the numerous innocent bloodshed, hatred, envy and malice between her people.

40 YEAR REVIVAL PROPHESHY GIVEN ON 3/10/2015

1. For 40 years beginning from 2017 – 2057, I will give Uganda spiritual vibrancy and economic prosperity to disciple nations but 2016 is the determining year for laying the foundation of the destiny of Uganda. 2016 will open the door for economic deliverance and economic revival in the land.

2. If Uganda slumbers and does not obey My word, instead of greatness, there will be a wilderness experience for 40 years where the disobedient will expire
3. If you obey My word, then nations will turn to me and your sons will be fathers to many nations
4. Seek me now and you will find me and I will instruct you and guide you to the place or nation that you will impact and disciple.
5. I will show my wonders, signs and miracles that will amaze the world. Kings, presidents and rulers will bow to you and listen to the word of God.
6. Persecutors will become dumb and amazed by the authority and power you display
7. Uganda is to help and travail for other nations that are incapacitated by idol worship and those disabled from knowing the Lord

THE BONDAGE HOLDING THE NATION OF UGANDA

Your ancestors sold you to the rulers of this dark age, the princes of your lands, to the gods of your tribe, clan and family. Some people have been dedicated to evil spirits by blood covenants, human sacrifice, circumcision and animal sacrifices. Businesses as well have been dedicated to evil powers as people searched for wealth and in turn unending circles of poverty in families because the evil powers have open contact to the financial sources.

Child dedications, initiation rites that involve cuttings on the skin created contact point where by their initiations has given Satan an access point to trace them up at any time.

Dedication has taken place through the following

1. The practice of witchcraft where by our fore fathers consulted familiar spirits, mediums, enchanters, witch doctors, astrologers, fortune tellers and they did great abominations before the almighty God. Women who have gone to witches to strengthen their marriage or seek for a child end up being molested sexually at the shrines. This has brought the curse of immorality, adultery and divorce in their generations.

2. Sacrificing to the ancestors things like animals, fouls, produce of the field has made spirits to control and interfere with their prosperity

3. Rituals performed during traditional ceremonies like giving of names, circumcision, funeral rites has directly initiated the people and given access to the evil spirits to haunt their lives.

All the above has ushered in the Jezebel spirit that strongly manifests itself in the form of;

- Increased witchcraft
- Poverty
- Immorality and prostitution
- Drunkardness
- Hatred and murder
- Lust
- Adultery
- Premature death
- Divorce

- Polygamy
- Pornography
- Gay/lesbianism
- Indecency

Arise oh my servant, repent and cry for mercy and deliverance from the Lord. Entreat forgiveness from the Lord for your generations. For I have purposed to lift up my standard in the nations to raise up an army to challenge the Jezebel spirit and to subdue the rulers of darkness in this age.

Stand in the gap and lift up your cry and proclaim liberty to your generations so that my servant may be set loose from the covenant of their ancestors and then come and serve me, carry the gospel of peace to the nations.

Arise build my broken altars, consecrate a fast and call an assembly that you may serve the Lord in liberty. Arise my watchmen that are scattered in the offices, schools, businesses and farming. Stand upon your tower; give your eyelid no slumber until my servant is at liberty.

Behold when my servant Uganda will be set loose, I will gird up my strength to do a great work through my servant.

EASTERN UGANDA

Thus says the Lord

I have stirred up my jealousy for eastern Uganda, for the prince of darkness in eastern has covered my people's zeal long enough. I have stirred up my zeal to overthrow him that my glory may be revealed in the east. My children's cry has reached my ears.

My glory in the east shall make my name feared upto the west. Arise, men and women, for I have lifted up my standard in the nations. I seek for somebody that I may send to declare liberty to their generations in the east. Arise, old, young, rich, poor and gird up your strength, prepare ye to fight the prince of darkness in eastern Uganda.

From the lips of my young infants I will ordain my praise. Your young men shall carry my banners and I will send them both near and far to carry the good news to a place and nation where my name is not hallowed.

Those that obey my word shall prosper and flourish in their ways for I myself will water them from my sanctuary and they shall bear much fruit and I will give to them from my Spirit. But the unbelieving, disobedient shall be loathsome to me and the yoke of the prince of darkness in eastern Uganda will get tighter on their neck and generation and you will be corrupted by the wickedness of this Dark Age. My eyes shall abhor you and your cry shall no longer be of my delight.

My glory came down on eastern Uganda long ago and I have set my pillars there and my fear has swept through to the west. My servants were blinded by the enemy not to see my glory that is risen upon them. The prince of darkness in eastern Uganda has blinded my servants through the numerous traditional and satanic rituals, dedications and covenants made by your forefathers and even in this generation. So my people are being defiled such that bondage encircles them in order not to discern my seasons and visitations.

If my people called by my name shall arise and see my glory that is risen upon them, then will I also rebuild every broken wall in their land. I will also overthrow the prince of darkness in eastern Uganda.

Consecrate fasts unto me in your generations and cry for mercy from the presence of the Lord and repent for the abominations of your generation. After all this I will revive my mercy unto you and I will cause you to proclaim liberty in the nations and then shall you also become my commissioned messengers to all nations both small and great. A people shall come trembling from far to inquire and to learn the fear of the Lord from you.

Come out from the traditions of your tribe, family and clan. Consecrate yourself and be holy to me. Cast behind you hatred, malice, injustice. Respect the grace that I have put upon each one of my servants. Stop the pointing of finger amongst you the family of God.

Come out of selfishness, begin to carry the burden of your nation, your brothers, family and your generations. Wake up my watchmen and slumber no more because I have purposed to perform my word in these days.

SHAKING EASTERN UGANDA PROPHESY
During a conference I was ministering in Malaba town in September 2016 at Divine Rescue Church hosted by Pastor Wanjala, God gave me a prophesy that a revival will break out in three years' time in Eastern Uganda and Malaba will be a fountain head that will affect eastern Uganda and western Kenya. Specifically in the month of June 2017 an event will take place to awaken people in eastern Uganda. This year from around March till June a draught has been experienced coupled with the invasion of armyworms that has devastated eastern Uganda most and other parts of Uganda too. There is famine, failed harvest, unproductivity as well as suffering among the people as poverty stings the land.

God is shaking the land and awakening the people to seek Him and renounce their evil ways because he wants to deal with the giants that struggle over eastern Uganda people. Wake up child of God for the Lord will yet shake the land more until the people rise to seek Him for the cause of the Kingdom of Heaven.

TO THE YOUTH

Gird up your strength and look to me you redeemed. In your youthful vigour, I will make you messengers, my apostles to near and distant lands. You shall travel from sea to sea and go from strength to strength.

Prepare ye the way for the Lord in your life that you may serve me with all your strength, mind and soul. I will lift up the infants and the youth to lift up my banner in the nations. Time has run out, arise from darkness that Christ may shine in you.
Awake you fornicator
Awake you sexually immoral
Awake you liars
Awake you double minded
Awake you adulterers so that your evil ways do not ensnare you
Awake to righteousness and let your garments and hands be clean

You who say you are sinning because you live in a corrupt world, behold on the judgement day Joseph will stand to challenge your excuse, for he withstood all the temptations of Potiphar's wife and escaped from adultery. You who say you are too young to serve the Lord, my servant Samuel will rise to challenge and testify against you on the judgement day. For as an infant the Lord called him and he responded to serve Him. Awake and deliver yourself from excuses and let my light shine upon you, let my glory be revealed through you.

When you obey and serve me, I will heal your land and make you a prosperous generation. All that I purpose in my heart to do to you will be unfolded. But if you disregard my call, you shall be ensnared by your own way and your own iniquities will destroy you and your bondage will get tighter.

INSTRUCTONS

1. CONSENCRATE FASTING AND PRAYER FOR THE NATION
2. RISE TO YOUR CALLING AND INVEST YOUR TIME AND RESOURCES IN IT.
3. MARRIAGES AND FAMILIES BE ALIGNED TO THE WORD OF GOD FOR I PURPOSE TO USE FAMILIES MIGHTILY.
4. WATCHMEN TO FOSTER PRAYER NETWORK TO GENERATE THE SPIRITUAL CLIMATE THAT WILL USHER IN REVIVAL.
5. PERSONAL HOLINESS, REPENT OF KNOWN SINS THAT HAVE BECOME A HABIT IN YOUR LIFE, BEHOLD MY EYES HAVE SEEN IT AND I DETEST IT.
6. UNITE FOR THE CAUSE OF THE HEALING OF THE LAND.
7. EVANGELIZE, EVANGELIZE AND EVANGELIZE.

UGANDA PROPHETIC POLITICAL TIMELINE

THE 1978 ORACLE AND FULFILMENT

From 1978 when President Idd Amin put a ban on the operation of all other Denominations, with the exception of Islam, Anglicans and Roman Catholic Churches, many Spiritual Leaders especially Pentecostal Churches went into exile and the Churches operated under ground because of the terrible persecutions.

Many Spiritual Leaders of the banned Denominations and Christians were either killed or Arrested and Imprisoned.

In Aug.1978, when the body of Christ consisting of Ugandan Exiles and Kenyan Christians were Praying and interceding for peaceful leadership in the Nation of Uganda, God spoke Prophetic words concerning the Political events that would soon begin to unveil themselves in Uganda hence warning the body of Christ to Stand in the gap for the Nation of Uganda.

GOD'S DECLARATION CONCERNING THE POLITICAL EVENTS IN UGANDA SINCE AUGUST 1978 TO DATE

A Minister of God from Kenya prophesied by the spirit of God that:

1. **Prophecy One:**
   Through the war that had started at Mutukula, Uganda-Tanzania border, the Ugandan exile and African liberation Army will join hand and overthrow the Government of Idd Amin in Uganda.

2. **Prophecy Two:**
   The First President will be an Elderly person and he'll be in power for a very short time and he will be overthrown.

3. **Prophecy Three:**
   The next President who will come after this first one will stay for a short time but relatively longer than the first one and he'll also be overthrown.

4. **Prophecy four:**

The Nation of Uganda will enter in a period of confusion after the overthrow of the second President. The Nation will have no President during this time until when an elderly man will become the President of Uganda.

5. **Prophecy five:**

This third President, (the elderly man) will rule Uganda for a relatively longer period, but during this period there will be confusion and bloodshed and there will state of Emergency in some part of Uganda until when he'll be overthrown again.

6. **Prophecy Six:**

The Prophecy Number six ushered UGANDA in the regime of the "Young Man" whose regime would be long and seemingly peaceful. "After this period, there will come a young man who would rule Uganda for a long time. During his rule the Country will seemingly be peaceful but not absolutely there will seem to be order and Development". This young man is non-other than the current President Yoweri Museveni Kaguta. This Prophecy began its fulfilment in 1986 to date.

7. **Prophecy Seven:**

The last Prophecy that has not yet been fulfilled is the Prophecy of Bloodshed during or after the period of young man. "After this period there will yet be bloodshed then the country will enter into real peace".

FULFILMENT OF THE ABOVE PROPHESIES:

Prophesy one:

A conventional war was officially launched against Uganda by the African National Liberation Army, which consisted of Ugandan Exiles and Armies from other African Nations In August 1978. This was backed up by International Nations such as Britain, Israel, and America, France to mention but a few. This war led to the overthrow of Amin's Government in Uganda on April 1979. This fulfilled first Prophecy.

Prophecy Two:

The first President who was put to power by African National Liberation Army and the International backups was Professor Yusufu Kironde Lule an elderly man who was in power for sixty days (60) only and he was overthrown. This fulfils the second Prophecy which stated that "The first President after the Liberation war would stay for a very short time."

Prophecy Three:

President Lule was succeeded by Godfrey Binaisa Lukongwa who was in power for 365 days (one year) and he was put under house arrest by Paulo Muwanga who was the Chairman of Military commission who ruled from May 12th – May 22nd 1980. This fulfils the prophecy number three that the second President in power for a short time but relatively longer than the first".

Prophecy Four

The Military Commission ruled Uganda under the Instruction of Dr. Apolo Milton Obote who was still in exile in Tanzania by this time because the International body especially the

Europeans Nations did not approve of him coming back to Uganda as leader. And he was not ready to come back to Uganda as a common man either.

Prophecy Five
The reign of Obote II begun in 1981 soon after the election and this regime was categorized as a period of fear, terror and bloodshed. In Kampala there was "Pandagari" (This was a time when Armies moved with Lorries picking men and young Boys from House to house at night and took them to be slaughtered in an attempt to destroy Museveni's Rebels who were busy attacking and raiding Police Posts and Armoury.

They killed innocent Civilians who neither had protection from Government nor the Rebels. In Central region, Area affected were Wandegeya, Makerere, Kikoni, Bwaise, Kawempe and all other Sububs of Kampala. While this happened around Kampala, Museveni's Rebels were terrorizing Luwero, Hoima, Kagadiya, Kigorobiya and others.

In West Nile Region, starting from Madi Okolo up to Arua through to Koboko and Moyo there was terrible massacre for two good years from 1981-1982.

This period of bloodshed in different part of Uganda fulfils the Prophecy that, this third President, (the elderly man) will rule Uganda for a relatively longer period, but during this period there be will be confusion, bloodshed and state of emergency in some parts of Uganda until when he'll be overthrown again.

The last part of this period of confusion was when the Acholi under the Command of Tito Okello Lutwaa and Bazilio Olara Okello overthrew the Government of OBOTE II in 1985, which they accused of favouring the Langi only and this overthrow now gave room for MUSEVENI to wage open war against the government because he successfully split and weakened the Army of Obote II.

As Soon as TITO Okello Lutwaa came to power, Museveni now waged open war against the Government of TITO Okello Lutwaa this war which started in 1980 continued through up to 25th January 1986 when he took over Government from TITO Okello Lutwaa.

Efforts to organize peace talk between TITO Okello Lutwaa and Museveni for the good of Uganda was to no avail because Museveni breached peace talks by matching his Army against the Government troops who had observed the cease fire.

Prophecy Number six:
This ushered UGANDA in the regime of the "Young Man" whose regime would be long and seemingly peaceful. "After this period, there will come a young man who would rule Uganda for a long time. During his rule the Country will seemingly be peaceful but not absolutely there will seem to be order and Development". This prophecy began its fulfilment in 1986 to date.

Much as this Prophecy seem to have brought the peace to UGANDA, some part of the country have suffered Political insurgencies to the extent that local people ironically have lived in camps in their own Villages for the last 30 years of this seemingly peaceful regime.

Prophecy Seven
The last Prophecy that has not yet been fulfilled is the Prophecy of Bloodshed during or after the period of young man. "After this period there will yet be bloodshed then the country will enter into real peace".

CONCLUSION

The call for Uganda.
Praise God my dear beloved of the most high, surely Uganda, God loves us. Every Prophecy that God gives through his Ministers is a warning to prepare us for Warfare against the evils declared in the Prophecies. Having done all to stand let us continue to against this last bloodshed and deny HELL the blood of UGANDA. Travail to produce the time of real peace as prophesy seven is being fulfilled

THE JUBILEE PROPHESY AND IMPLEMENTATION
Many people in Uganda today are complaining and pinpointing fingers concerning political leadership of the nation but God has His purposes at stake and therefore has a special interest in the nation of Uganda.

Prosperity and political muscle of western Uganda does not originate from man's clever schemes or geniuses but a divine promise. This is what God said, "because your forefathers welcomed the Gospel with an open heart, prayed for, catalysed and ushered in the East African revival, I the Lord heard their prayers" One of the old men who was a revivalist in western Uganda prayed for blessing and prosperity. The Lord told him that he will not see it during his generation because he is a pioneer but it will come to pass in the generation of his sons and grandchildren. "Now I have given the current generation a Jubilee gift of 49 years of prosperity, blessing" But the national leadership was to prepare and open doors for the blessing and prosperity but not forever.

1986 A.D is the 120th jubilee from Adam therefore it is a prophetic season for western Uganda. The liberation of Uganda in 1986 is God's jubilee for Uganda. President Museveni's coming coincided with a season of jubilee and fulfilment of God's promise to the revivalists of western Uganda. So the president came to power in 1986 at a prophetic timing of the nation of Uganda. When President Museveni finishes his jubilee mandate (which I cannot disclose in this book for security and confidentiality reasons) he will "rest." And then the prophesy number seven (7) on the political timeline of Uganda will be fulfilled.

The leadership of the nation, the blessings and the opportunity associated with it has been given to western Uganda this time due to the prayers of the revivalists as a gift for allowing God to use them.

"I have not given them because of the current leaders or individuals but according to my promise to your forefathers says the Lord". The revivalists laid a prayer and faith foundation that has the capacity to subdue principalities that interferes with the presidential office and major arms of government (Executive, Judiciary and legislative). Various tribes and people may struggle for power but if they do not have prayer, faith and spiritual capacity to uphold that office, God cannot trust such a group. Uganda is special nation to God chosen for the revival of the latter day harvest and to disciple nations.

The Lord told me He gave West Nile the opportunity for 8 years to rule the nation but their son closed churches, killed, practiced witchcraft and sorcery. "They followed after their own heart and served other gods and no one upheld him and his office in prayer. So I turned away my face from them and took away what I had given them. They lost favour with me and they were ignored for many years until they remained backward in many things and lost opportunities for their destiny in God. They paid a high price including wars, bloodshed and loss of their own sons and daughters over the years. Any leader who persecutes the church and despises God's work will not prosper or stay in leadership in this nation of Uganda"

"I also gave the people of Lango and Acholi national leadership but they did not seek me but followed their own heart and served other gods. I also took leadership and all opportunities that came with from them.

Their land suffered judgement; they paid a high price with their blood"

"Watch out Western Uganda because I see confusion, division, selfishness, greed, fights amongst you where an evil atmosphere is being created. Let the intercessors arise to stand in the gap to uphold the Jubilee gift. Let churches unite to open channel for revival in the land" West Nile and Acholi and Lango regions have lost and regretted the divine opportunities they were given which they could not sustain. As for you rise up to uphold the Jubilee gift before it is taken away from you"

"I have brought west Nile back to my limelight after afflicting her and chastising her over her sins but I now kindle a fire of revival and strength to birth prosperity and destiny of nations"

Let's first understand the laws of Jubilee and redemption

The Law of Jubilee
"And Jehovah spake unto Moses in Mount Sinai, saying, Speak unto the children of Israel, and say unto them, When ye come into the land which I give you, then shall the land keep a Sabbath unto Jehovah. Six years thou shalt sow thy field, and six years thou shalt prune thy vineyard, and gather in the fruits thereof; but in the seventh year shall be a Sabbath of solemn rest for the land, a Sabbath unto Jehovah: thou shalt neither sow thy field, nor prune thy vineyard.

That which groweth of itself of thy harvest thou shalt not reap, and the grapes of thy undressed vine thou shalt not gather: it shall be a year of solemn rest for the land. And the Sabbath of the land shall be for food for you; for thee, and for thy servant and for thy maid, and for thy hired servant and for thy stranger, who sojourn with thee. And for thy cattle, and for the beasts that are in thy land, shall all the increase thereof be for food. And thou shalt number seven Sabbaths of years unto thee, seven times seven years; and there shall be unto thee the days of seven Sabbaths of years, even forty and nine years. Then shalt thou send abroad the loud trumpet on the tenth day of the seventh month; in the Day of Atonement shall ye send abroad the trumpet throughout all your land. And ye shall hallow the fiftieth year, and proclaim liberty throughout the land unto all the inhabitants thereof: it shall be a jubilee unto you; and ye shall return every man unto his possession, and ye shall return every man unto his family. A jubilee shall that fiftieth year be unto you: ye shall not sow; neither reap that which groweth of itself in it, nor gather the grapes in it of the undressed vines. For it is a jubilee; it shall be holy unto you: ye shall eat the increase thereof out of the field. In this year of jubilee ye shall return every man unto his possession." (Leviticus 25:1 – 13)

Leviticus 25 explains the law of Jubilee as well as the law of redemption. If a man in Israel lost his land through poverty and debt, he had to work for others to repay his debt. But no matter how far into debt he went, he would always return to his land inheritance at the end of the Jubilee cycle (49 years).

Leviticus 25:54 says, and if he be not redeemed in these years [of servitude], then he shall go out in the year of Jubilee, both he and his children with him.

This is grace at its highest level. No man can go so far into debt that he cannot be redeemed by grace in the end. The Jubilee not only allows it; it demands it. We know that there are many who have not appropriated the redemptive grace of Jesus. What is to become of them? Are they doomed to remain in bondage to Master Sin forever? No. The law has a "statute of limitations" on sin and debt bondage. This is the law of grace. It is manifested and demanded by the law of Jubilee, so that even if they are not redeemed during those years of servitude, they must be set free at the Jubilee purely by an act of grace.

Law of redemption

"And if a sojourner or stranger wax rich by thee, and thy brother that dwelleth by him wax poor and sell himself unto the stranger or sojourner by thee, or to the stock of the stranger's family; After that he is sold he may be redeemed again; one of his brethren may redeem him: Either his uncle or his uncle's son may redeem him, or any that is nigh of kin unto him of his family may redeem him; or if he be able, he may redeem himself. And he shall reckon with him that bought him from the year that he was sold to him unto the year of Jubilee; and the price of his sale shall be according unto the number of years, according to the time of an hired servant shall it be with him..." Leviticus 25:47-53.

The debtor who is redeemed is to serve his redeemer "as a yearly hired servant" (Lev. 25:53). In other words, the redeemer buys the servant's debt note. The servant simply changes masters and now works for his near kinsman. He is not free in the absolute sense, even though he has been redeemed. The above law of redemption requires a brother or near kinsman to redeem the person in bondage.

Signs to show our current President is a jubilee president
There are things commanded in the jubilee and redemption scriptures above which President Museveni fulfilled and qualifies him to be a jubilee resident.
1. People were liberated from oppressive governments and tyrannical, brutal security forces through the liberation war
2. People returned from exile;
   a. Kabaka returned from exile.
   b. Ugandans who took refuge in other neighbouring countries returned.
   c. Political exiles returned to Uganda
   d. Indians returned to Uganda
3. Some political prisoners were given pardon and set free
4. Properties of people were returned to them
   a. The land was taken away by previous regimes and was returned to the people by the 1995 constitution
   b. Indian properties were returned to them
5. Traditional Kingdoms which were abolished by tyrannical government were restored
6. Graduated tax and its crude way of collections were scrapped off.

7. Freedom of worship was granted to all Ugandans and church denominations which were abolished by the dictatorship governments were restored.
8. Freedom of press was granted
9. Amnesty was granted to former rebels groups and individuals which abandoned rebellion
10. Universal primary and secondary education was granted to promote education of the poor
11. Prosperity for all program launched
12. As a brother or close kinsman he redeemed Ugandans by paying with his own life and the life of others in the liberation wars that cost them a lot.

The above are signs to prove beyond doubt that he fulfilled the conditions and requirements of a jubilee year. After completing his assignments, the president's jubilee mandate will be over and then God will allow him to leave leadership and allow another worthy leader to take over and consolidate the jubilee achievements of the nation that are in place.

This Jubilee prophesy is not to be taken as a promotion for His excellency President Yoweri Kaguta Museveni but an explanation to help clear some political dilemmas some people have over the political timelines for Uganda. I have both good news and bad news for him concerning how he is handling his Jubilee assignments and when the assignments will be over (which I cannot disclose in this book due to confidentiality and security of our nation but face to face with him, I can let him know all of it as the Lord spoke to me). Whoever targets me over this revelation to harm or sabotage, his generation will be like Eli's and Ahab's family.

CHAPTER FOUR
Nations Revival Prophesy
Kenya 04/10/2016

THE THREAT

In my vision I saw a black smoke rising from the coast of Mombasa blanketing the entire nation of Kenya. The darkness of the smoke filled the whole nation and immediately many events begun to take place.

First the church leaders begun to have conflicts which led to splitting of churches the church conflicts caused hatred, division, blackmail, court cases, fleshly fights in the churches. Secondly the pastors and church leaders begun to die of complicated diseases that have no cure and the churches begun to be paralysed.

Thirdly, the fervent intercessors begun to die also of complicated sicknesses and so much reproach was heaped on the churches because of these sicknesses killing pastors and intercessors.

The church prayer power went down and the body of Christ in Kenya became vulnerable to satanic manipulation as the agents of Satan begun to take up city by city in the nation.

The Kenyan parliament begun to pass laws which are contrary to the operations of the church and ministry to the point that the government begun to contradict the will of God.

The terror attacks were accelerated by the enemies of the nation since the church's prayer power went down.

There was drought in the entire Bungoma County which led to famine. Rain fall ceased for a very long time and crop yields deteriorated and farming was paralysed.

Intercessors and Pastors of Bungoma were the first to begin to die in the nation because that is the first area targeted by the agents of the devil in their agenda to bring down the church in the nation. The demons recognised that there are strong servants of God in Bungoma who are not popular but strong spiritual pillars in the nation.

Servants of God begun to abandon Bungoma area and fled to other comfortable areas in the nation and others left ministry to go and look for survival.

Finally the judgement of God came down on the nation as the church was spectating the events that were happening (Ezekiel 22:30)

INTERPRETATION
The black smoke that rose up to cover the whole nation was a satanic ritual that was done at Mombasa by key satanic

principalities and agents in Kenya. They had a meeting where they complained that the church in Kenya is rising and making their work difficult and therefore a drastic measure had to be undertaken. They came up with the following resolutions

- A living human sacrifice was to be offered and burnt alive
- A ritual was to be performed on the person to be sacrificed and this ritual was to put spells, tragedies, embargoes, limitations and terminate the church leaders, intercessors and the influence of the churches in the nation.
- The person was to be burnt alive and the smoke from the burning sacrifice would then pollute the spiritual, social, political and cultural atmosphere of the nation so that the church is suffocated and the nation captured in Satanism.
- They concluded that Bungoma County will be their first target because there are servants of God and intercessors who are upholding the nation in prayer and many of them are pillars that hold the nation in spiritual realm.
- After Bungoma, Nairobi is next and then other towns and cities are to follow.

DIVINE PURPOSE OF THE VISION

The nation of Kenya in three years' time from October 2016 will begin to experience revival. The centre of this revival is western Kenya and Bungoma is one of the fountain heads of this revival that will sweep through the nation.

Bungoma is a spiritual pillar that holds the entire nation of Kenya followed by Nairobi.

The attack will first hit Bungoma so that it can be paralysed so that the revival is crushed. This revival will restore the Glory of God and righteousness in the nation so that lost souls will be harvested into the Kingdom of God. There will be demonstration of God's power and miracles through His chosen and faithful servants.

For a long time the occult powers have drawn people after idolatry by performing signs and wonders through false prophets and cultic leaders who claim to come in my name when I have not sent them.

I will make a distinct difference between those who truly serve me and those who do not serve me and yet claim to represent me.

THE REMEDY

Call to action

1. The intercessors and pastors/church leaders are to call prayers in the nation in all the regions, counties, towns and districts to establish a prayer cover that can destroy the evil plan and save the nation from disaster.
2. The body of Christ needs to come in unity and work together to extend the kingdom of God in the nation. Stop the infighting and pointing of fingers on one another and promote brotherhood of all tribes as a people equal in Gods sight and living in covenant relationship with God.

3. Missionary intercessors need to be recruited, trained and sent to infiltrate all territories of the nation of Kenya to implement an apostolic and prophetic prayer cover.
4. Release of the fivefold ministry and Disciple the nation
5. The principality called Kilimanjaro that rules over East Africa is resident in Kenya and must be brought down and dethroned.

Blessings for obedience

1. When you will obey, then I will deliver the nation from all the evil schemes of the enemy and establish my banner of deliverance in it.
2. There will be peace and economic prosperity enjoyed by the citizens
3. You will be my chosen apostles to go and deliver distant lands and bring hope to the lost
4. Your children will eat the good of the land
5. Your voice will be heard in the nation and you will impact the nation and turn it to me

Judgement for disobedience

1. All the calamities spoken in here will come to pass
2. You shall become a laughing stock and an example of judgement
3. Famine, conflict, calamities will hit the nation
4. The church will be handcuffed by the nation
5. Demonic religions will be promoted to overshadow the church
6. There will be a generational gap in the church

SOUTH SUDAN PROPHECY
THE BURDEN
In 2014 I got a burden to pray for South Sudan for spiritual awakening and political stability. In 2015 the body of Christ in Arua began to pray for the nation of south Sudan concerning the conflicts and political instability that led to loss of many lives. Through this time God kept on speaking about the nation and its people groups.

When south Sudan got independence from Sudan through the referendum, the nation was supposed to enter a season of jubilee and practice the jubilee principles so that national development could start on a foundation of freedom and godliness but the nation focussed on power, wealth and luxury as well as individual benefit among its halls of power.

VISION OF REVIVAL
On 3rd October 2015, during a season of prayer from 21st September to 1st of November, I saw a fire burning in Uganda – West Nile and this fire took three paths. The fire was a fire of revival and one path went northwards through South Sudan, Sudan, Egypt. From Egypt it divided in two, one went to Asia pointing to India and another went to Europe pointing to Netherlands.

South Sudan is on the path of a Revival that will shake Africa and spread to the nations of the world. But this revival is hindered by the state of the nation at hand. The nation is in pain, disunity, hatred and war that have claimed many lives.

There is an evil covenant that is hindering the nation of South Sudan from progressing in the destiny of the nation.

THE STATE OF THE CHURCH AND THE NATION

In my vision I saw the map of the nation of South Sudan but from the borders of the nation and the interior was looking like a wilderness. There was a small area that had a city in the centre and some green scenery and all people gathered to stay there.

In the vision we were asked to walk through the wilderness and pray so that there will be a change. We saw empty river valleys and there was no sign of water. We were to pray so that rivers will again begin to flow in the wilderness in order to make the land blossom with life again. We obeyed and went into the nation praying through our journey until we reached where the people were living.

We were startled to see that where people lived, they did not care that the wilderness is closing in on them but continued to live luxurious lives. We saw people busy buying new cars, building and buying houses, buying new clothing, having leisure and fun. We were told not to stop but pray for the towns and continue to the north.

When we reached the north we met two brothers fighting each other. They used to love one another so much that they stayed together, worked together, ate together and helped each other. But they had a conflict where they split and hated one another to the point that one wanted to commit suicide in front of us but the other brother did not care.

We were asked to finish our prayer journey over a mountain where the covenant of love was made between the two brothers. We were asked to go with banners of love and fix them as flags on that mountain to conquer hatred and disunity. When we succeeded to fix the flag or banner of love, the brothers came to their senses and reconciled with each other and danced together.

INTERPRETATION
The conflict in South Sudan is turning the nation into a wilderness experience but the church and the people of God are relaxed and everybody is trying to take sides in the conflict and do what others who do not know God are doing. Many are living in luxury and others are planning to leave the nation to avoid the conflict. They have not paid a price for their nation in love to lay down their lives with fasting and repentance to the Lord.

People are focussing on their own development, welfare and luxury as the nation is sloping into darkness and gloom. The Gospel of the Kingdom of God is not supported and facilitated to reach unreached communities.

The brothers who hated each other represent people who are filled with greed and selfishness and fighting one another which later will lead to national calamity. Brothers are killing each other, tribes are turning against one another and slowly the nation is turning to a wilderness and a place of reproach.

The mountain on which the banner of love is fixed represents the hatred, unforgiveness, murder, tribalism, segregation. All these can only be overcome by love but not guns. When the nation will turn to God and repent of their sins and love one another as the Lord Jesus commanded, there will be reconciliation and one day brothers, tribes and clans will dance together in the praise of God almighty on the same platform.
It is time to seek the Lord and lay down your lives for the redemption, deliverance and healing of South Sudan.

THE EVIL COVENANT HOLDING THE NATION
In my vision in May 2016 I saw a gathering of two tribes of South Sudan in an open field. An old man with grey hair sat in the middle and on his right was the Dinka tribe and on his left the Nuer tribe. In the vision I saw some horrible things happening between the two tribes being induced by the old man.

Whenever the old man lifted up his right arm, immediately the Dinka tribe would attack the Nuer tribe and as he lifted his left hand, the Nuer tribe attacked the Dinka tribe and this went on for a long time until the two tribes begun to diminish in number, power and strength.

INTERPRETATION

The old man represents an old ancestral tribal covenants that the founding leaders of these two tribes made with a principality and a spiritual deity to be guardian ruler and defender. The conditions of the covenants were as follows;

The covenant with the principality or deity

- The spirit or principality will receive worship, honour, allegiance and human sacrifice from the two tribes.
- The spirit r principality will be chief ruler over the tribe as the tribal chiefs submit to them
- The principality will give power, protection and prominence to these tribes to be above all other tribes in power, rule and influence.
- That the two tribes will service the altars of this deity by continually making war with other tribes, looting, killing as a way of obtaining sacrifice.
- That the tribes will never directly rule but the deity will rule over them

Covenant of brotherhood between the DINKA and the NUER

- These two tribes had a covenant of brotherhood between them that they will defend each other; love one another and work together to become a prominent people in the nation and among the tribes.
- They agreed not to fight one another but promote each other's welfare.

Breach of covenants and judgement

- The first generation that made this covenants died and many generations came after and the current generation does not know the existence of such covenants and its terms.
- When the tribes did not service the covenants terms and the altars became dormant, the evil spirit and principality begun to attack, confuse and destroy the two tribes by inciting them against each other so that the bloodshed will be a forced sacrifice to the deity they covenanted the people to.
- When South Sudan separated from Sudan and became a nation, the evil principality maintained its dominance, influence over the nation since the covenant stated that it will be the supreme leader and not a human being. As a result that spirit has caused confusion, disunity, hatred, segregation, tribalism and bloodshed.

GOD'S JUDGEMENT

- The wrath of God has come over the nation because the nation has been involved in idolatry, witchcraft, innocent bloodshed
- The blood of people killed in the conflicts and sacrifices to the deity are crying to God for vengeance
- The nation will continue in bondage, captivity and exile if they don't repent and turn to the almighty God
- There will be a wilderness time of hunger, famine and scarcity that will paralyse the economy of the nation
- But if the nation repents and turns to God, there will be restoration, revival and national development.

ASSIGNMENT AND MANDATE
1. Establish a national prayer cover
2. National repentance and covenant breaking
3. Altars of God in the land
4. Release of the fivefold ministry and Disciple the nation
5. Unity in the body of Christ

NIGERIA

PROPHESY ON THE NATION OF NIGERIA GIVEN ON 13/03/2017

1. The 3rd wave of revival is going to hit Nigeria and there will be a ground breaking awakening that will shake West African nations.
2. There will be soul winning, healing, economic recovery that will last for 40 years. This year 2017 is a year of the beginnings of birth pangs
3. The killing of the Christians and bloodshed of the saints is preparing ground as a catalyst for multiplied harvest of souls and the move of revival.
4. There will be a scenario of the Macedonian call from nations (Acts 16:9-10). Europe is the Macedonia that is calling Nigeria for help.
5. Missionaries will be sent from Nigeria with the power of God to deliver and release Europe. Blessings will pour back to the nation.
6. If you obey and rescue Europe, I will hear the cry of your nation and fulfil her destiny but if you do not obey, your nation will continue in turmoil and be vandalised.

EGYPT PROPHECY

"The season has come for my revival fire to hit Egypt. I shook the gods of Egypt like I did in the days of Moses. Now Egypt will lift up my banner of salvation and worship me in homes, streets, and hold up holy days unto me. Egypt is my door to the east and gateway to Asia and Europe and I have established my highways there to reach my people and lift them out of affliction and slavery to idols and turn their hearts to me so that I will heal them says the Lord" "My trumpet shall sound in you and my name shall be hallowed by babes, young men and fathers and my fame will be evident in the land"

What does the Bible say about Egypt? In Isa 19:19-25 a)
a. There will be an altar to the Lord in the heart of Egypt. Vs 19
b. A monument to the Lord Almighty in the land of Egypt.
c. A sign and a witness to the Lord Almighty in the land of Egypt.
d. They will cry to the Lord and He shall send them a Saviour/ defender, he will rescue them.
e. The Lord will reveal Himself to the Egyptians. Vs 21
f. He will strike and heal them. Vs 22
g. A highway will be there from Egypt to Israel. Vs 23
h. Israel will be third, along with Egypt and Assyria "a blessing to the earth". Vs 24
i. The Lord Almighty will bless them saying 'blessed be Egypt my people, Assyria my handiwork, and Israel   my inheritance.' Vs 25

j. Second time God will reclaim/draw a remnant that is left of this people from Assyria from Lower Egypt, Upper Egypt, from Cush from Elan.

k. People from beyond Ethiopia will acknowledge Him as Lord, Zep 3:10,

l. They will worship with sacrifices and grain offerings. Isa 45:14

m. Princes shall come out of Egypt. (Africa). Ethiopia shall soon stretch out her lands unto God. Ps 68:31 (KJV)

NAMIBIA PROPHECY

My hand is over Namibia as my messenger of revival and renewal in southern Africa and a gateway to America. I will make your scorching deserts to blossom with life giving Spirit to revive the souls of my people. Prepare ye the way of the Lord in Namibia, arise and speak my word without fear. I am about to do a thing in Namibia that will cause nations to southern Africa to flock in to receive and witness.

My signs and wonders will be seen and millions of souls will be won to Christ and many lives healed and transformed. I will heal your ancient wounds and cause you to praise and rejoice with the joy of the Lord. Your land will be blessed and your children will dwell securely.

Come out of wickedness and renounce sin and hatred from among you so that my hand will be upon you to lift you up. I am about to clean my house in Namibia to prepare for a visitation.

The unclean will be judged but the righteous will flourish like a fruitful vine. Am preparing myself to visit Walvis bay to turn it into my tabernacle of worship and discipleship of nations.

SENEGAL PROPHESY

A voice of mourning and wailing is heard in Senegal, smoke, turmoil and petitions from the people. The Lord is visiting Senegal to purge out all that persecute and trample my salvation under feet. Repent and be converted so that times of refreshment and restoration will come on you.

I have heard the cry of my people who believe in, I will arise to rescue them from persecution and I will make the houses of the persecutors like the house of Jeroboam son of Nebat who led Israel to sin. I have my people in this nation that worship me and honour me with their life. I will restore and bless them. Fear not but mention my name in the nation and make my works known so that I may redeem my people held captive by sin and religion.

GHANA PROPHESY

Thus says the Lord, I have made you a model, a father, a mentor and a classroom for Africa. I gave you peace so that you may proclaim my name and raise a standard for baby nations so that through you I may set model nations and excellence national governance.

Because of your peace, there is a rising complacence among your people and my mandate was forgotten and now the nations in Africa languish in fatherlessness as well as the church. Arise and shine for the season of revival has come.

CENTRAL AFRICA PROPHECY

You are wounded and torn apart by hatred, bloodshed and pain. But I am opening my hands to you to receive you, to heal you and to establish you. Repent of the bloodshed, hatred, revenge and malice so that your land may stop speaking against you before me because of the blood. My Judgement on wickedness will continue until the nation turns to me and honours me with their worship and life.

I have a purpose to use you in these last days to take the good news to unreached people groups in Africa as my chosen vessel. Arise, repent and shake yourself from the dust and trust me for you establishment. Turn to me and be blameless in my sight and I will use you mightily in these last days for a great harvest of souls. Prepare ye the fivefold ministries in the land and empower my people.

CALIFORNIA PROPHECY

I am kindling a new awakening in you to revive America in these last days. My fire in America has been snuffed out by wickedness and my altars are full of ash but no fire burning. Arise and blow the trumpet in the nation of America. You are my pillar and weapon to restore the fear and knowledge of God in these last days. Turn away from iniquity and sin that easily entangles. Fear not but be courageous to challenge evil.

Judgement looms on the nations of America for rejecting my ways and bending to ways that are contrary to my ways and upholding the wisdom of men and disregarding my righteousness. Arise do not delay to pray, intercede and proclaim my counsel in America.

ASIA PROPHECY

I have purposed to trample the idols of Asia in a soon coming contest between me and Asian idols in an open display of my glory and greatness. I have held my peace long enough. I have been training my sons in Asia for this great day. The sons of Asia will rise and lift my banner in the land and courageously proclaim me before rulers and content with the forces of darkness that held Asia captive.

India is my hot spot for shaking Asia with the knowledge of God. I have raised prophets in Asia who will confront evil like Elijah confronted Ahab and the prophets of Baal. My fire is kindled to display my glory in Asia. Repent, turn from wickedness, renounce idolatry and turn to me for I am prepared to contend for the lost souls bound in idolatry in Asia.

EUROPE PROPHECY

Europe is fallen and the knowledge of the Holy one is cast out. There is a Macedonian call from Europe (Acts 16:9-10) for help. Europe has rejected the knowledge of the Holy one. My sword of judgement is drawn out to judge Europe. By 2020 if Europe does not repent and return in my ways, there will be calamity, insecurity, bloodshed that will devastate Europe. For all that rejects God and offends His holiness is given room in Europe.

Arise intercessors of Europe and cry for mercy for time is running out for the people in the nations of Europe. The sons of Africa will be sent to Europe to spearhead revival and disciple Europe to return to God in these last days.

AFRICA PROPHECY

INTRODUCTION

Africa is a continent of about fifty sovereign states. Many countries of Africa especially the Northern Africa are predominated by Islam and this were not in earlier centuries.

In the OT, Israel's main concerns in Africa were naturally with their powerful neighbour, Egypt. She had changing roles as the granary of the Patriarchs, the oppressor during the bondage or the broken reed of the period of Assyrian advance. Despite the cruel past, a tender feeling towards Egypt remained (Dt. 23:7), which prepares us for the prophecies of Egypt's eventually sharing with Israel, in the knowledge and worship of the Lord (Isa 19: 1-25. Other

African people are mentioned from time to time (Libya and Put), but most frequently allusions are Cush (Ethiopia), the general designations for the lands beyond Egypt.

At some periods historical circumstances linked Egypt and Ethiopia in Hebrew eyes, and they stand together, sometimes with other African peoples, as representative nations on which God's judgments will be executed. (Isa 43:3, Ezk 30:4-5, and as those who will one day receive Israel's God. (Ps 87:4 & 68:31).

The picture of Ethiopia, symbol of the great Africa unknown beyond the Egypt River, stretching out hands to God was like a trumpet call in the missionary revival of the 18th and 19th centuries. Even within the biblical period it had a measure of fulfilment; not only where there were Jewish settlements in Africa (Zep. 3:10) but an Ethiopian in Jewish service did more for God's prophet than the true-born Israelites (Jer. 38: 7-13), and the high-ranking Ethiopian of (Acts 8:26-39) was evidently a devout proselyte.

This description of Africa helps us to see that in the Bible, Africa is represented by Egypt, Cush or Ethiopia.

With a better understanding of where our continent is and where we are destined to be in God's purpose, we will with the help of the Lord cause our continent to arise and go her destiny. Let's do a biblical search to locate Africa in God's purpose for nations.

In Isaiah 19:1-25 especially the first four verses, Africa is described as;

- An object of scorn.
- Africa is despised.
- Africa has debts that are heavy and will be paid for a long time by the coming generations.
- The truth is that we have devastating wars in Africa that last for many years and conflicts between each other e.g. Angola, Namibia, Rwanda, Burundi, Ethiopia, Somalia, Sudan, DRC, Zimbabwe and Kenya etc.
- Famines in many African countries
- Diseases, epidemics of Ebola, HIV and AIDS.
- Poverty

What is Africa's hope?

When God created the world, He created Africa. God has a purpose for Africa. God has had no dealings with any other continent as He has with Africa. God's purposes still stand for Africa. What the Bible says about Africa in Old Testament and New Testament is that;

1. It's a wealthy place; it is a store house of God. Genesis 2:10-12,
   a. Exodus 12:35-38
   b. Exodus 35:5-7
2. It is a place of refuge
   a. Genesis 12:10- 20 Abraham in times of famine came to Egypt.
   b. Genesis 42 – 46 Jacob and his sons went to Egypt in time of famine.
   c. Mathew 2:13-23 Jesus Christ our Lord as a baby found refuge in Egypt.

3. It is a training ground
    a. Genesis 39:1-23, Joseph was trained in Africa to
       conserve the resources of Egypt.
    b. Genesis 41:41-57 Joseph in charge of Egypt.
    c. Exodus 2:1- 11 Moses was born, raised and trained as a
       leader/Saviour of the Israelites in Africa
    d. Joshua was also born in Egypt and he became a leader
       after Moses.
4. It is accepted in intermarriage with Israelites and
    offspring adopted by Jacob.
    a. Genesis 41:45 Joseph married an African wife Asenath
       daughter of Potiphera priest of On.
    b. Genesis 41:50-52 Manasseh and Ephraim were born to
       Joseph by his wife Asenath.
    c. Genesis 48:5&6 Jacob adopted Manasseh and Ephraim
       as his own sons and blessed them.
    d. 1 Chronicles 7:20-27 Joshua commander of God's army
       hailed from Ephraim. Many judges and prophets came
       from Ephraim.
    e. Moses married an Ethiopian wife and God defended
       her when Miriam and Aaron rose against her. Exodus
       2:21, Nu 12:1-2.
5. It is a place of battle: God manifested His power in Africa
    more than anywhere else. God's war with Pharaoh greatly
    demonstrated His power which made Him famous not only
    in Africa but entire human race. Africa became a
    confrontational ground (Ex 7-12).

In Egypt Moses fought battles in FOUR realms of power where there were many gods. In each battle Moses dealt with a different god. These realms are:-
   a.   The Heavenlies - The sun was turned into darkness.
   b.   Hailstones came to spoil their crops.
   c.   Moses dealt with the sun god and the god of thunder.
   d.   The Earth – dust, flies, locusts, livestock and boils.
   e.   The Waters - Water was turned into blood and frogs came out of the water. He dealt with the water spirits.
   f.   The Occult – When Moses' snake swallowed the other snakes he dealt with occult powers.

Africa in the New Testament
   a.   Jesus as a baby found refuge in Africa in Egypt. Mat.2: 13-23
   b.   Jesus was helped to carry His cross to Golgotha by Simon the Cyrene. Cyrene was a small village in Libya then. (Lk 23:26)
   c.   The Gospel came to Africa first through Philip as he preached and baptized the Ethiopian eunuch. Acts 8:26-40 d) On the Pentecost day, people were there from Africa too. Acts 2:1-13
   d.   Among the prophets and the teachers; Lucius of Cyrene was there. Acts 13:1
   e.   When the church was prosecuted. Among those who were preaching in Acts 11: 19-20 Cyprus, Antioch some were from Cyrene.

Prophesy of God is coming to Africa in scriptures
See the Lord rides on a swift cloud and is coming to Egypt. The idols of Egypt tremble before Him and the hearts of Egyptians melt within them, (Isa 19:1).

We must prepare this continent for God's visitation. God has a purpose for Africa. Before his purposes are fulfilled we need to do a work of preparation in every African nation. All the sins that defile the land must be repented of and prophetic prayers done.

- The doors of righteousness must be opened for God to come.

- The old decrees of our nation must be cancelled and new decrees written.

- Every other God must be dethroned and the Lord Jesus must be enthroned.

AFRICA REVIVAL PROPHESY

1. I will use AFRICA in these last days as a gateway to usher revival and awakening to the nations and this revival will shake the world in these last days.
2. There will be economic deliverance and economic revival in Africa
3. The wealth of Africa that have been taken during the colonial eras will be poured back through the nations Africa will touch during the revival.
4. I have raised Apostolic fathers in Africa whom I will send to disciple and father nations.

5. Africa will send and sponsor missionaries to other nation in this season of revival.
6. God is raising Apostolic and prophetic ministries to spearhead and lead this revival.
7. There will be massive soul winning and church planting for the next 40 years.
8. Africa is my midwife for the tangible supernatural manifestations in these last days.
9. Africa is a multiplier of seed

INSTRUCTION

1. Establish personal, corporate and prayer altars for nation's destiny to intensify the spiritual climate.
2. Train and raise the fivefold ministries to be deployed to collect and manage the harvest
3. Raise up Apostolic and Prophetic intercessors to become territorial commanders to govern the revival protocols
4. Unite ministries and body of Christ in the nations to manage the revival

CHAPTER FIVE

How God Deals With Nations On Jubilee Principles

BLESSED TIME

Every nation is given the 490 blessed time or "grace period" to enjoy prosperity and peace. 490 = 70*7 forgiveness Jesus talked in the bible for number of times you forgive a sin of somebody when Peter asked him about forgiveness in Mathew 18:21-22. 490 blessed time principle governs the patience, forgiveness and grace of God. 490 is a period of ten (10) jubilees. This is the basic unit of measure in long term Bible prophesy. It surfaces only three times in the Bible Genesis 4:24, Mathew 18:22, Daniel 9:24.

The jubilee principle in the Old Testament represents the Grace principle of the New Testament. All nations have their Jubilee period where God cancels their debts or gives them total deliverance or grace. But the New Testament Grace is activated by repentance which caused God to relent from judging us but instead extends to us undeserved favour.

Jesus illustrated the jubilee principle with a parable in Mathew 18: 21-35 about a king who forgave a debt of 10,000 talents after the grace period expired.

The servant repented (begged for mercy) or interceded and the king cancelled the debt. But the same man met his neighbour who owed him a smaller debt but refused to forgive him and threw him to prison and sold his family into slavery to fully pay his debt. When the king heard it He reversed the debt cancellation and threw the man in prison.

When a nation receives God's Grace due to the repentance and intercession of her people, it enters its triple inheritance of eternal life, prosperity and divine destiny. But if that nation sins and turns away from God oppresses its people, neighbours and does not lift up the vulnerable people, they regress into a time of Judgement which is called cursed period.

Jesus was not just talking about the monetary debts but trespasses and sin. The parable is an illustration of the principle of seventy times seven (70 x 7). One might say the debt was paid after 490 days. This parable shows us how the principle of jubilee works in a practical way. This is a kingdom parable that shows us how God deals with nations and people groups.

THREE RESTS FOR NATIONS

There are three rests in the law

1. The 7th day where everybody, animals, servants, slaves were to rest completely
2. The 7th year which was rest for the land where no one sowed or reaped (Lev 25:4-5) except the poor could

reap and eat what grew by itself (Exo 23:11). All oxen were at rest, all Hebrew servants were given one year's vacation from servitude (Exo 21:2).

3. The Jubilee rest (7 x 7 years) where all debts are cancelled and everybody returned to his inheritance. The jubilee ends all servitude, and all men were able to begin on a clean slate, debt free. This is the greatest rest of all the three. In the first two, debts are held in abeyance for either a day or a year. They are released temporarily but not forgiven fully. The jubilee after 49 years is when all debts are permanently released.

So when a nation is birthed by getting independence through a revolution or liberation war or peaceful referendum for freedom, it begins its 490 grace period or blessed time period.

Jesus saw that the people were not practical on the jubilee principle so instead of the 49 year jubilee he took it to ten jubilees to help them grasp the principle. He did this to reveal hidden Bible prophesy principle most people don't grasp today.

HOW GOD JUDGES A NATION AFTER 490 TIMES OF OPPORTUNITY FOR FORGIVENESS ELAPSES
Illustration with nation of Israel
If an individual Israelite sinned against God or becomes unclean for any reason, he is to bring sin offering in the Temple to atone for his sin.

The blood of the animal is poured under the altar to dispose his sin and the priest does this for many and the Temple becomes more defiled by the sin on its ground throughout the year. So once a year, the high Priest once a year on the Day of Atonement offers a sacrifice and brings the blood to the holy of holies to sprinkle it on the mercy seat of the Ark of the Covenant. In so doing he obtained forgiveness, atonement and mercy for the nation.

God forgave the nation of Israel once a year or 49 times every jubilee cycle or 490 times every ten jubilees. Under normal circumstances God forgives a nation 490 times before the time of accountability comes to determine whether to extend another grace period depending on people standing in the gap for such a nation. This is the greatest reason for an intercessory network for a nation. If no intercessory prayers are made for a nation whose 490 times of grace period is ended, God will judge that nation. But if people stand in the gap for that nation God will extend the grace period for that nation for another 490 times. In other words, repentance and maintaining a covenant status God starts with them all over again. We have seen this again and again in the book of Kings how God judged wicked kings and started all over again with the righteous ones.

To illustrate His answer about forgiveness, Jesus started the parable in Mathew 18:23-24 by saying " therefore is the kingdom of God likened unto a certain king (God) which would take account of his servants. And when he had begun to recon... "

In other words the king (God) had forgiven 490 times over and it was times of reckoning. He is obligated to forgive a nation 490 times (Grace period) before reckoning the debt (sin) of that nation. Many people have missed to understand this way God deals with the sins of nations.

GRACE PERIOD, JUDGED PERIOD AND CURSED PERIOD FOR NATIONS

These are jubilee related terms and we will look at them individually for better understanding.

1. Grace Period (blessed time) - this is the 7 x 7 = 49 or 70 x 7 = 490 year period leading to jubilee, the 10,000 talent debtor in Jesus parable which represents the nation of Israel when we apply this principle on a national level. It should be noted that this 49 Or 490 years grace period applies to nations that are obedient to Gods law or word or have a covenant status. In other words it is applicable to Gods servant. The debtor in Jesus parable in called the kings servant therefore the king does not reckon until the 490 times of forgiveness ends.

2. Cursed period - However not all nations make efforts to serve God and they cannot be rightly called God's servants. Nations which for one reason or another become liable for obedience to Gods law, but which remain deliberately rebellious and disobedient are not given a full grace period of 490 years instead their grace period is shortened to 400 years which is called

cursed period. This is actually a period where God gives the nation opportunity for repentance before reckoning it's debt (sin). This can be illustrated by the way God dealt with the Canaanite nations that did not serve Him hence they were not entitled to a Jubilee opportunities. This is illustrated in Genesis 15:12-16.

And when the sun was going down, a deep sleep fell upon Abram; and, lo, an horror of great darkness fell upon him. And he said unto Abram, Know of a surety that thy seed shall be a stranger in a land that is not theirs, and shall serve them; and they shall afflict them four hundred years; And also that nation, whom they shall serve, will I judge: and afterward shall they come out with great substance. And thou shalt go to thy fathers in peace; thou shalt be buried in a good old age. But in the fourth generation they shall come hither again: for the iniquity of the Amorites is not yet full.

3. Judged period - This is a period for a nation that delayed its obedient and therefore late for a full grace period. This specifically applied to Israel who was supposed to enter the Promised Land in a period of two years but 10 of the spies sent to spy the land gave an evil report causing the people to lose faith. The results were disastrous for them. God prohibited them from entering the land for another 38 years. Thus God forbade them for 40 years not to enter the land.

For this God would now reckon their debt (sin) on a 490-40 = 430 years rather than giving them a full 490 years.

When Israel was given the law at Sinai the day was thereafter commemorated as the feast of Pentecost. Approximately 490 was the 50th jubilee from Adam, when the 12 spies gave their report. If the Israelites believed Caleb and Joshua's report and entered the Promised Land, they would have entered in the grace period or blessed time. Not only would their decisions be made based on the 490 year cycle, but they would have returned to their inheritance on the 50th jubilee from Adam (50 x 49 years). Unfortunately they entered the Promised Land late, and their grace period was shortened to just 430 years.

All this reveals that God deals with nations in three different grace periods.
1. Grace period (490yrs) or blessed time for nations that serve the Lord
2. Cursed period (400yrs) for nations that do not serve the Lord
3. Judged period (430yrs) for nations that have delayed their obedience and hence late.

CHAPTER SIX

Strategy for Effective Intercession

THE WATCHMAN AND THE FOUR CLAIMS

"I will stand my watch and set myself on the rampart, and watch to see what He will say to me..." (Habakkuk 2:1).

For thus the Lord said to me: "Go, set a watchman; let him announce what he sees. When he sees riders, horsemen in pairs, riders on donkeys, riders on camels, let him listen diligently, very diligently."

Then he who saw cried out: "Upon a watchtower I stand, O Lord, continually by day, and at my post I am stationed whole nights. And behold, here come riders, horsemen in pairs!" And he answered, "Fallen, fallen is Babylon; and all the carved images of her gods he has shattered to the ground." O my threshed and winnowed one, what I have heard from the LORD of hosts, the God of Israel, I announce to you. The oracle concerning Dumah. One is calling to me from Seir, "Watchman, what time of the night? Watchman, what time of the night?" The watchman says: "Morning comes, and also the night. If you will inquire, inquire; come back again" Isa 21:6-12.

"Principles from the above scriptures

- A rampart is defined as "a wall-like ridge."
- Habakkuk spoke of setting himself on the rampart (or wall) to watch. Notice he said, "I will stand my watch..."
- He considered this a personal assignment. It was his specific time to "watch," and he was determined to be faithful.

An intercessor as a watchman takes personal responsibility to

- To see what is coming forth
- To announce what he sees
- Listen diligently
- Stand upon watch tower continually
- Announces oracles from the Lord concerning nations
- Announces times and seasons
- Makes inquiries of the Lord and gives responses to inquiries from people

THE FOUR CLAIMS OF A WATCHMAN'S PRAYER

1. **Claim One: Open Doors!**

The watchman/intercessor needs to decree open doors so the Gospel can be freely proclaimed in their region or nation. "Devote yourselves to prayer...that God may open a door... so that we may proclaim...Christ" (Colossians 4:2-3, NIV).

2. **Claim Two: Open Minds!**

The watchman/intercessor needs to decree or command minds to open so people will hear the Gospel with an open mind.

"I am sending you to them [the lost] to open their eyes and turn them from darkness to light" (Acts 26:17b-18a, NIV).

3. **Claim Three: Open Hearts!**

The watchman/intercessor needs to decree a heart of flesh or soft hearts so unbelievers will invite Christ into their hearts. "For God...made his light shine in our hearts to give us the light of... Christ" (2 Corinthians 4:6, NIV).

4. **Claim Four: Open Heavens!**

The watchman/intercessor needs to decree open heavens so the transformation of a culture may begin.
"Open up, O heavens, and pour out your righteousness. Let the earth open wide so salvation and righteousness can sprout up together"
(Isaiah 45:8, NLT).

THE 12 PRAYER STRATEGIES THAT MOVES NATIONS Introductory thoughts

1. Nations are built on systems and institutions
2. The systems and institutions are built on the pattern of principalities
3. The people run the systems and institutions but the systems and institutions control the people
4. Demonic principalities infiltrate the systems because they are friendly to luciferian agenda and use them to control the people.

5. Religions are constantly infiltrated and run by systems of a nation and as a result they fail in their mandate.
6. The church of Jesus Christ is busy dancing on the Babylonian stage and enjoying its delicacies while forgetting their prophetic role.
7. God's dominion agenda will flourish on the Kingdom dominion strategy which was designed by God to beat the luciferian agenda.

Below are kingdom principles for effective intercession for a nation's destiny

1. Religion (The Church, Ministries, and Other Faiths)
Ephesians 3:14-21, Ephesians 1:15-23
- Pray for the Holy Spirit's anointing on all churches no matter their denomination.
- Pray for ministries involved in evangelism and discipleship including foreign missionary activity.
- Pray for all faiths and religions that they will see the truth of the Gospel of Jesus Christ.
- Pray that Christians will be bold in their witness.
- Pray for revival

2. Family and Marriages (Youth, Children, Marriages, etc.)
Ephesians 5:25-33, Mark 10:1-9, Genesis 18:17-19,
Pray for the peace of Jerusalem—Psalm 122:6.
Psalm 47:1-3 (NIV)
Clap your hands, all you nations; shout to God with cries of joy. For the Lord Most High is awesome, the great King over all the earth......He subdued nations under us, peoples under our feet.

- Pray for families in general, and particularly the healing of broken relationships in marriages and families, especially among believers and those in Christian ministry.
- Pray for the sanctity of marriage.
- Pray against cultural influences that diminish the value of marriage and family.
- Pray for a godly heritage
- Pray for children and their salvation and godly upbringing

3. Education (All Schools, Universities, Colleges, and Educators)
Ecclesiastes 12:9-14, Proverbs 1:5-9, Psalm 33:10-11 (NIV)

The Lord foils the plans of the nations; he thwarts the purposes of the peoples......But the plans of the Lord stand firm forever, the purposes of his heart through all generations. This focus involves all institutions of education, whether for the very young, when children are so easily influenced, or those studying at higher levels.
- Pray for teachers and educators.
- Pray for those you know by name. Add them to your daily prayer lists for each day.
- Pray also for the content of textbooks so they will reflect biblical values.
- Ask God to send a revival to all campuses.

4. Business (The Marketplace)

Isaiah 60:1-6, Deuteronomy 8:18-20, Psalm 45:5-6 (NIV)

Let your sharp arrows pierce the hearts of the king's enemies; let the nations fall beneath your feet. Your throne, O God, will last for ever and ever; a sceptre of justice will be the sceptre of your kingdom.

- This focus involves praying for a spiritual awakening in the marketplace.
- Pray especially for Christian businessmen and women that God will use them to influence others in their professions.
- Pray for major corporations that they will build their companies on a foundation of high moral and ethical standards.

5. Government (Local, National, and International)

Romans 13:1-7, 1Timothy 2:1-4, Psalm 22:27-28 (NIV)

All the ends of the earth will remember and turn to the Lord, and all the families of the nations will bow down before him, for dominion belongs to the Lord and he rules over the nations.

- Pray for heads of your local, state (or province), and national government.
- Remember especially to intercede for the judiciary (judges) of your nation and all other arms of government
- Include the military of the nation and law enforcement as well as other service officials, such fire fighters and civil servants.

- Intercede for other nations.

6. Media (The Press, Television, Internet, and Social Networking) Ephesians 2:1-7, Mark 7:17-23 Psalm 45:17 (NIV)

I will perpetuate your memory through all generations; therefore the nations will praise you for ever and ever.
- Ask God to cause all aspects of the media and information technology to become a tool in His hands to change the culture around us for His honour and glory.
- Pray that the influence of the Internet and social networking will be used by Christians to capture a new generation of young believers.
- Pray that Christian values and ethics will find their way into all aspects of the media.

7. Arts and Entertainment (Including Sports)
Ephesians 4:17-24, Philippians 4:8-9, Psalm 46:10-11 (NIV)
"Be still, and know that I am God; I will be exalted among the nations, I will be exalted in the earth."......The Lord Almighty is with us; the God of Jacob is our fortress.
- This focus includes all those in any field of the arts or entertainment including sports.
- Some have defined this sphere as the "Celebration" sphere because it takes many such aspects into consideration.
- Ask God to use the influence of those who know Him in these arenas so they might impact many around them.

- Pray for entertainers or athletes you know by name who have a strong Christian testimony. Ask God to expand their influence.

8. Health care and Science

Exodus 15:23-26, Jeremiah 33:6-9 (Doctors, Nurses, and Medical Professionals)

One of the great needs in the nations concerns adequate health care. Sadly, many of the diseases in the world, especially in less developed nations, are preventable or easily treated with proper medicines and hygiene.

- Pray today for those who do not have adequate medical care and for those who have a heart to help meet this need in our nation and the nations of the world.
- Ask God to use Christian doctors and nurses not only to minister to the physical needs of their patients but to the spiritual needs as well. especially pray for those involved in medical missionary enterprises as they often risk contracting the very diseases they seek to treat.
- Pray "by name" for doctors, nurses and other medical professionals you may know.
- Pray that those who are followers of Christ in more blessed lands will make themselves available as frequently as possible to use their unique gifts to help the sick and suffering in the nation. In this way they will help fulfil God's promise of Psalm 72:12: "For he will deliver the needy who cry out, the afflicted who have no one to help" (NIV).

9. The Economy

Leviticus 26:3-12, 1 Timothy 6:5-10 (Banks, Lending Institutions, and Greed)

The uncertainties of the economy affect all of us in different ways, including those ministries that seek to spread the Gospel globally.

Very often mission's organizations are the first to suffer in an economic slowdown.

- Pray for a healthy recovery in all sectors of the economy and that a spiritual awakening will take place that helps overcome the greed that caused so much of the recent economic woes.
- Pray also that if this is God's way of getting the attention of Christians to depend more on Him and to reject the ways of the world that a true revival will result. The great spiritual awakening of the 1850s, in which hundreds of thousands came to Christ, began as a result of a nationwide failure of America's banking system.
- In particular, as you serve as a watchman of the Lord today, ask God to allow Hebrews 13:5 to come alive in the hearts of His children: "Make sure that your character is free from the love of money, being content with what you have; for He Himself has said, 'I will never desert you, nor will I ever forsake you'" (paraphrase).
- More specifically, intercede for individuals you know of "by name" who have lost their jobs and are struggling financially as a result of a failing economy. Ask God to open opportunities for them to find meaningful employment.

- Additionally, pray that even amid these difficult
- times Christians will continue to give faithfully to
- their local churches and other worthy ministries.
- Pray also that those more blessed financially will be
- even more generous.

10. Pray for JUDICIARY

(The Courts and Judges of Our Nation and the Nations of the World)

Justice is defined as "the upholding of what is just; especially fair treatment in accordance with honour, standards, or law." It is to "treat adequately, fairly, or with full appreciation." The judicial branch of many governments is clearly one of the most influential of all aspects of authority.

Their decisions touch the life of every citizen and, when functioning properly, help protect individuals from exploitation, settle disputes, and punish criminals who break the law. In many parts of the world, however, such justice is hardly the norm. Judges and politicians are too often corrupt, and the result is injustice at all levels of society.

- Today we make this a matter of our fervent prayers. Ask the Holy Spirit to show you areas in your own nation or community where justice is desperately needed.
- Pray specifically for nations or areas of the world that you know to be lacking in administering true justice to people, especially those nations that op press women, minorities, Christians or the poor in general.

As followers of Jesus we should be model citizens who, "Defend the poor and fatherless; do justice to the afflicted and needy. De liver the poor and needy; free them from the hand of the wicked" (Psalm 82:3-4).

- Pray that God will raise up more Christian judges and lawyers locally and globally who are guided by honesty and truth.

Proverbs 2:1-9, Deuteronomy 16:18-20, Isaiah 51:4-5 (NIV) "Listen to me, my people; hear me, my nation: Instruction will go out from me; my justice will become a light to the nations......My righteousness draws near speedily, my salvation is on the way, and my arm will bring justice to the nations. The islands will look to me and wait in hope for my arm."

11. Prayer for ISRAEL

(The Well-Being of God's Chosen People)

The nation of Israel clearly plays a pivotal role in the history and destiny of nations. The Bible includes important promises that link our blessing and prosperity as believers to how we treat Israel. We are admonished to "pray for the peace of Jerusalem" and to speak blessing on the Jewish people (Psalm 122:6-9). God said through the Prophet Zechariah, "He who touches you touches the apple of His eye" (Zechariah 2:8). In the many prophecies of Scripture that point toward end times, it is clear that Israel is a central focus in much that transpires.

The apostle Paul set an example of praying for the Jewish people when he declared, "Brethren, my heart's desire and prayer to God for Israel is that they may be saved" (Romans 10:1).

- Today, in addition to all that we pray for during our time as watchmen, we pray for the peace of Jerusalem and seek a blessing on Jewish people everywhere.
- We especially pray for the eyes of God's chosen people to see the reality of their true Messiah, Jesus Christ.
- Pray particularly that God will strengthen Messianic Jews who are willing to endure suffering, as Paul did, for the privilege of proclaiming Jesus Christ to their fellow Jews.

Psalm 122:1-9, Zechariah 2:10-13 (NIV),
Psalm 47:7-8 (NIV)
For God is the King of all the earth; sing to him a psalm of praise. God reigns over the nations; God is seated on his holy throne.

12. PRAYER FOR YOU

Go, gather all the Jews to be found in Susa, and hold a fast on my behalf, and do not eat or drink for three days, night or day. I and my young women will also fast as you do.

Then I will go to the king, though it is against the law, and if I perish, I perish." Esther 4:16

Personal destiny prayer is key in preparing the intercessor for the assignment to disciple nations and confront or bring down giants that target prayer ministers.

- Prayer of consecration
- Prayer of dedication
- Prayer of communion
- Prayer of empowerment
- Prayer of warfare
- Strategic prayer

These prayers prepare the intercessor for duty

COMMANDING THE GATES OF THE NATION/CITY

Psalms 24:7 Lift up your heads, O gates, and be lifted up, O ancient doors, that the King of glory may come in!

Gates defined:
Purpose of gates:
1. A place for great assemblies of the people as they passed in and out of the city. Proverbs1:21
2. A place for public deliberation, debates, reading the law and proclamations. 2 Chronicles 32:6; Nehemiah 8:1-3 (government).
3. A place where the priests and prophets delivered their discourses, admonitions and prophecies. Isaiah 29:21; Jeremiah 17:19-20; Amos 5:10 (religion, media).
4. A place where business was carried on. 1 Kings 22:10, 2 Kings 7:1; Ezekiel 11:1 (7 mountains).
5. A place were legal transactions were conducted and witnessed. Genesis 23:10,18; Ruth 4:1-11(government).

6. A place where cases were tried and judgment pronounced. Deuteronomy 21:19; 22:15; 25:7-9; Job 31:21; Amos 5:16 (government).
7. A place for gathering news and gossip. Genesis 19:1; Psalm 69:12 (media).
8. A place that attracted the attention of the sovereign or dignitary at his going out or coming in. Esther 2:19, 21; 3:2 (7 mountains)

Figurative Expression:
1. Gates can represent the city itself. Genesis 22:17; 24:60; Ruth 4:1; Psalm 87:2; 122:2-3
2. The —gates of hades‖ in Matthew 16:18 is to be understood as all aggression by the kingdom of darkness against the Church.

TYPES OF INTERCESSORS AND THEIR RANKS
1. Face to face intercessors
They speak to God face to face as a man speaks to his friend. The examples are;
   a. Moses – Numbers 33:11-12, Numbers 11:1-8 b. Abraham – Genesis 18:16-33
   b. Paul
   c. Elijah
   d. Elisha
   e. David
   f. Simeon (Luke 2:25-36)

Governmental rank intercessors
a. They change and affect destinies of nations
b. They interact with arch angels (Gabriel and Michael

c. They fight principalities
d. They are above the rank of lions and eagles and whales.
e. They are masters of revelation

Example are;
- Daniel
- John the Baptist
- Isaiah
- Mordecai
- Nehemiah
- Esther
- Joseph

3. Prophetic intercessors
Prophetic intercessors are those who are called to prepare the way for God's will to be done upon the earth.
a. They carry nations and people in their heart b. They state answers
b. They birth destinies of people and nations
c. They are proclaimers and enforcers of divine decrees

Examples are
- Jeremiah (Jer 9:1; 20:7-9
- Habakkuk – (Hab 2:1-3
- Ezekiel
- Moses
- Joseph

4. Confrontational / frontline intercessors

a. They are tough warriors
b. They initiate battles in the realms of the spirit
c. They are territorial commanders
d. They destroy and disarm the spiritual forces of wickedness in the heavenly places
e. They dethrone principalities
f. They command chariots of fire and horsemen in the angelic realms

Examples are

- Deborah (Judges 4:1-7)
- Paul (Eph 6:10-12)
- Joshua (Joshua 10:12-13)
- Jehoshaphat, Man of War—Man of Peace (2 Chronicles 20)

5. Worship intercessors

a. They bring down the presence of God through worship
b. They turn and discern seasons of God by worship c. They are spiritual weather changers

Examples

- Hannah, a Profile in Worship Intercession (1 Samuel 1-2)
- Anna the widow – (Luke 2:37-38
- Jehoshaphat (" Chronicles 20:20-27)

6. CRISIS INTERCESSORS -

Paramedics of Prayer - Biblical
Example: King David, God's Crisis Intercessor

7. ISSUES INTERCESSORS

Stand Against Injustices - Biblical Example: King Lemuel's Mother (Proverbs 31) Description: Those who pray over issues will find that the Holy Spirit puts an assignment on their souls. Sometimes issues flow out of their own hurts; other times the Lord simply drops a burden like a seed into the heart's soil and then pours out prayers to water it.

8. SALVATION INTERCESSORS

God's Midwives – Biblical Example: Paul, God's Great Soul Intercessor (Paul's Epistles)

9. PERSONAL INTERCESSORS

Spiritual Guardians - Biblical Example: Mordecai, Esther 's Personal Intercessor (Book of Esther)

10. FINANCIAL INTERCESSORS

Faith for Funding - Biblical Example: Joseph, God's Financial Intercessor (Genesis 37-41)

11. GOVERNMENT INTERCESSORS

Watchmen for Politics and Church - Biblical Example: Daniel, a Prophetic Government Intercessor (Book of Daniel)

12. PEOPLE GROUPS AND ISRAEL INTERCESSORS

Prayer Shepherds for Ethnic Groups. Biblical Example: The Woman at the Well, a People Group Intercessor

13. APOSTOLIC INTERCESSORS

GODS TERRITORIAL COMMANDERS - Biblical example: Joshua and his prayer in Joshua 10, Paul in his prayer for the churches Ephesians 3:14-21, Ephesians 1:15-23

THE PRACTICE OF APOSTOLIC AND PROPETIC INTERCESSION FOR NATIONS

What is apostolic and prophetic intercession?

- Apostolic intercession consists of proclamations, declarations and decrees released with the objective to unlock God's Kingdom purposes on Earth.
- Prophetic intercession refers to stating answers and the end from the beginning of those things we desire to see or manifest. They are called to prepare the way for God's will to be done upon the earth. It is calling what is not as though they are

PROCLAMATIONS, DECLARATIONS AND DECREES

- Speaking forth God's intended word for Earth carries great power to perform His intended purpose.
- Words of authority, spoken in faith and power, release things that are in the Father 's heart but are not yet visible on Earth.
- Believers have the authority to enforce God's will on Earth through words of proclamation and decrees that cause God's already existing will to be released.
- Prophetic proclamations and declarations are not just words spoken into the air or written on a piece of paper.
- They are used to stop the works of the enemy and to release the blessings of God.

- Proclamations, declarations and decrees are weapons of warfare designed by the Lord to destroy onslaughts of wicked spirits.
- Believers speak words of power and authority as they know the will of God
- First we have to understand the will of God through the Word and the Spirit.

Prophetic proclamation:
Officially announce and make known publically what God says.

Prophetic declaration:
Officially pronounce authoritatively what God says.

Legislate:
To make or enact a law

Decree:
A formal order having the force of law...a judicial decision or order...one of the eternal purposes of God...to command, ordain, or decide by or as if by decree.

PROPHETIC PROCLAMATION TOOLS

POWER IN THE SPOKEN WORD

1. Mouth

Jeremiah 1:9 Then the LORD stretched out His hand and touched my mouth, and the LORD said to me, Behold, I have put My words in your mouth. Isaiah 49:2 And He has made My mouth like a sharp sword; In the shadow of His hand He has concealed Me, And He has also made Me a select arrow; He has hidden Me in His quiver.

2. Fire & Hammer:

Jeremiah 23:29 "Is not My word like fire?" declares the LORD, "and like a hammer which shatters a rock?

STEPS IN PROPHETIC PROCLAMATION

Isaiah 40:9 Get yourself up on a high mountain, O Zion, bearer of good news, Lift up your voice mightily, O Jerusalem, bearer of good news; Lift it up, do not fear. Say to the cities of Judah, "Here is your God!"

a. Set self upon a high mountain b)
    Lift up voice
b. Do not fear
c. Speak to the city, land, homes, bones and the breath of God

Bones: (Dry Conditions)

Ezekiel 37:4 Again He said to me, "Prophesy over these bones, and say to them, 'O dry bones, hear the word of the LORD.' Ezekiel 37:7 So I prophesied as I was commanded; and as I prophesied, there was a noise, and behold, a rattling; and the bones came together, bone to its bone.

Breath: (life and revival)

Ezekiel 37:9 Then He said to me, "Prophesy to the breath, prophesy, son of man, and say to the breath, 'Thus says the Lord GOD," Come from the four winds, O breath, and breathe on these slain, that they come to life."

Mountains: (impossibilities)
Ezekiel 36:1 "And you, son of man, prophesy to the mountains of Israel and say, 'O mountains of Israel, hear the word of the LORD.

Land: (Possessions   and inheritance)

Ezekiel 36:4 'Therefore, O mountains of Israel, hear the word of the Lord GOD. Thus says the Lord GOD to the mountains and to the hills, to the ravines and to the valleys, to the desolate wastes and to the forsaken cities, which have become a prey and a derision to the rest of the nations which are round about.

Lift up a hand or a banner

Isaiah 13:2 Lift up a standard on the bare hill, Raise your voice to them, Wave the hand that they may enter the doors of the nobles.

PROPHETIC PROCLAIMERS AND POSTMEN INTERCESSORS

We have to become proclaimers of the Oracles of God instead of being postmen intercessors. Oracle proclaimers are the Prophetic intercessors who enforce Gods Agenda while the Postmen intercessors are mere delivery agents.

Difference between Oracle proclaimers and Postmen

POSTMEN
They deliver messages to people without knowing the content of the message apart from the address on the envelop, they have no right to open the envelop and hence no power to enforce the message's fulfilment.
1. Postmen deliver mail in a passive sense.
2. They come to your house and drop off what they believe is for you.
3. They have knowledge of your address on the letter.
4. They know enough only to tell you if it is from the electrical, cable or water company, but however, they lack the inside scope.
5. Many intercessors called to operate in a prophetic anointing settle for the postman anointing.
6. Their revelatory insight is like that of the postman, and they can only discern what is on the surface, therefore their prayers are not as effectual as they could be.

ORACLE PROCLAIMERS

Mathew 2:1-3 – a Decree was issued by Caesar Augustus for the whole world to be registered. But this decree was taken to all region by proclaimers and people responded without Caesar going personally to enforce it because the proclaimers have the Kings authority and sceptre in their hands.

1. Oracles proclaimers are heralds sent with authority from a king or ruler, their role is important.
2. They declared with authority what was happening or what was to come, and they did so from a place of being both informed and under authority.
3. They spoke what the ruler wanted to be said, and not what they thought should be said.
4. They had a sceptre (Staff or Rod) in their hand, which conveyed their right to decree as a sent one (Apostolic) from the king, and their knowledge of the details was immense.

Even so, we are called as intercessors to stand in the gap as;
- Apostolic (sent ones),
- Prophetic (informed) oracles of God.
- We make decrees - Jesus said in Matthew 16:19, that we have been given the authority to bind and loose by our decrees. In Luke 10:19, He reminds us that we have also been given all authority over the enemy.
- We are proclaimers, Matthew 10:27, Jesus again reminds us that what He has told us in secret we are to herald/proclaim upon the housetops.
- We make declarations, (John 11:43) Jesus didn't beg the Father to please wake up Lazarus so he could get another shot at life. No! Jesus proclaimed and demanded in a loud voice, "Lazarus, come out!". fervent prayers are not begging prayers, but they are declarations that are filled with divine insight into a situation and its outcome. Therefore one doesn't beg God for something to turn out a certain way, but rather one makes the decree of what will happen, based on prophetic insight.

As you can see, praying the voice of the Lord is not confined to one's vocal chords, but it is a yielding of one's complete self to the Lord so that He can use you for His glory. As God's intercessor, don't create reservations about the moving of the Spirit of God, but yield to Him, and you will see great fruit in your ministry.

The role of apostolic - prophetic intercessors
1. They are proclaimers of God's word and counsel
2. They are enforcers of divine decrees
3. They revoke decrees of destruction and

DECREES:
Decree defined:
a. A formal order
    - an authoritative direction or instruction; command.
    - conformity or obedience to law or established authority
b. Having the force of law
    - Principles and regulations established by a government or other authority and applicable to a people, whether by legislation or by custom en forced by judicial decision.
    - Any written or positive rule or collection of rules prescribed under the authority of the state or nation, as by the people in its constitution
    - An act of the highest legislative body of a state or nation.
    - Any rule or injunction that must be obeyed
    - An order given by one in authority

c. To ordain, to enact or establish by law, edict, etc.
d. To decide by, to solve or conclude (a dispute) by
   awarding victory to one side

Principles of decrees
- Decrees were written in the languages of all it concerned.
- Decrees were written in the name of the king
- Decrees were sealed with the king's signet ring
- Once a decree is made and written into law, it cannot
  be revoked
- Another decree could not revoke the previous
  decree

Examples of decrees in the Old Testament
Esther 1:19
Esther 3:8-12
Esther 8:8-11

Decrees were also in New Testament times
Luke 2:1 Now it came about in those days that a decree went
out from Caesar Augustus, that a census be taken of all the
inhabited earth. NAS

CHAPTER SEVEN

Fresh Encounter

In the year that King Uzziah died I saw the Lord sitting upon a throne, high and lifted up; and the train of his robe filled the temple. Above him stood the seraphim. Each had six wings: with two he covered his face, and with two he covered his feet, and with two he flew. And one called to another and said: "Holy, holy, holy is the LORD of hosts; the whole earth is full of his glory!" And the foundations of the thresholds shook at the voice of him who called, and the house was filled with smoke. And I said: "Woe is me! For I am lost; for I am a man of unclean lips, and I dwell in the midst of a people of unclean lips; for my eyes have seen the King, the LORD of hosts!" Then one of the seraphim flew to me, having in his hand a burning coal that he had taken with tongs from the altar. And he touched my mouth and said: "Behold, this has touched your lips; your guilt is taken away, and your sin atoned for." And I heard the voice of the Lord saying, "Whom shall I send, and who will go for us?" Then I said, "Here am I! Send me." Isa 6:1-7

The Invitation

Many churches and Christians despair over the increasing sinfulness of their communities and nations. The world gets darker and darker, pervasions are on the increase and what used to be ungodly and criminal is being legalized and accepted as norms and orientations, good morals are trampled under feet by lifestyles and legal systems. This moral and spiritual decay in the nations also happened in Isaiah's days.

The problem really is not with the darkness but the problem is with the light because when light shines, it dispels darkness. Jesus calls us to let our light shine and in this case we have been invited for a fresh encounter with the Lord just as Isaiah encountered Him.

Isaiah's fresh encounter with the Lord in the Temple started as a terrifying experience because in this same Temple the Lord struck Uzziah with leprosy but here Isaiah's life changed and we can learn from his experience to have our own encounter. The following is manifested in a fresh encounter;

- God revealed His holiness
- Isaiah became so afraid and aware of his sinfulness
- Isaiah confessed his sin in sincere repentance
- God forgave Isaiah, forgave him and removed his guilt by cleansing him
- God announced His mission for which He needed a messenger
- Isaiah in his revived state immediately volunteered
- God commissioned him to "Go and tell this people..."

This is a pattern that is still valuable for us to have a fresh encounter even in a sinful nation and respond to God's mission of reconciling the world to Himself.

There is a sense of urgency as God is calling Uganda to spearhead a great revival and our dry lives, altars and hearts need a fresh encounter to get a better perspective and boldness to move on in this calling. The encounter starts with your life before the other people come in view and there should be a thirst and a hunger in your heart for this to become a reality (John 7:37-38, Isaiah 55:1-12, Rev 22:17, Mal 3:7, Acts 3:19)

God's Plumb line

A plumb line is used to measure a strait wall during construction. God used in scripture the idea of a plumb line to describe how His people have rebelled or departed from Him and they are no longer aligning with Him. his is what he showed me: behold, the Lord was standing beside a wall built with a plumb line, with a plumb line in his hand. And the LORD said to me, "Amos, what do you see?" And I said, "A plumb line." Then the Lord said, "Behold, I am setting a plumb line in the midst of my people Israel; I will never again pass by them; (Amos 7:7-8)

What God measures here is not how much we have worked for Him but how we relate with Him. He created us for intimacy and personal love relationship with Him. The most important commandment according to Jesus is to love Him with all that we are, our mind, soul, strength (Mark 12:30). In this relationship, God reveals His power and might.

Sometimes you may have a relationship with God but your church as a body may depart from the ways of the Lord because of condoning sin and wickedness. So when we move out of fellowship with Him, he disciplines us because He loves us. Many people and churches can get familiar with sin that it takes discipline to bring them back in love. His messages to the seven churches in Revelations is a plumb line because they were not aligning straight to His measurement. This is a time to personally return to the Lord and love Him with all your being.

The Radical U-Turn
We need a radical change in our lives, practices, laws and faith to redeem our nations and bring them to their destiny according to the Lord's purposes. But this radical change starts with us in obedience to what the Lord has called us to do. You have to separate from evil and respond to your call and assignment in your own generation. Jonah first ran away from His call until God trapped him in a desperate situation but finally he radically made a U-Turn to go where he was sent and later the people he was sent to also radically changed.

Then the word of the LORD came to Jonah the second time, saying, "Arise, go to Nineveh, that great city, and call out against it the message that I tell you." So Jonah arose and went to Nineveh, according to the word of the LORD. Now Nineveh was an exceedingly great city, three days' journey in breadth. Jonah began to go into the city, going a day's journey. And he called out, "Yet forty days, and

Nineveh shall be overthrown!" And the people of Nineveh believed God. They called for a fast and put on sackcloth, from the greatest of them to the least of them. The word reached the king of Nineveh, and he arose from his throne, removed his robe, covered himself with sackcloth, and sat in ashes. (Jonah 3:1-6)

Ahaz was a wicked king who shut the house of the Lord and worshipped other Gods until the Lord's anger and judgement came on him and the people. But when his son Hezekiah became king, he sought the Lord for forgiveness and reopened the temple and restored worship and sacrifices and the Lord healed the people. (2Chronicles 30:6-27). This radical U-Turn brought revival and restoration in the land because one person radically changed.

Many other people like King Josiah, Nehemiah, and Ezra made a radical change and turned their people back to the Lord's ways and the Lord hearkened unto their prayers and brought prosperity, joy, restoration to the people. You need a radical decision to turn your life wholly to God without stumbling blocks and compromises.

The New Covenant People
"But you are a chosen race, a royal priesthood, a holy nation, a people for his own possession, that you may proclaim the excellencies of him who called you out of darkness into his marvellous light. Once you were not a people, but now you are God's people; once you had not received mercy, but now you have received mercy. (1Pe 2:9-10)
God has a new covenant with His new Israel (church) to be

royal priests and a holy nation. God's people are special treasure to Him because we have a relationship with Him and He has called us to redeem a lost world to Him.

We are a royal priesthood. This means all believers have access to Him king of kings and we are part of the royal family by adoption as sons. The priest's role was to stand between God and the people to mediate and that's our assignment to stand in the gap between God and humanity.

We are also a holy nation, which means we are set apart for special use. We are to separate from wickedness, worldliness and be different as salt and light of the world. We are His co-workers and therefore reflect His nature.

Prepare ye the way for the Lord
When God comes in revival, He comes with a refiner's fire which burns all impurity to accomplish purity. He will start with the sins of the nations in the church.
"But who can endure the day of his coming, and who can stand when he appears? For he is like a refiner's fire and like fullers' soap. He will sit as a refiner and purifier of silver, and he will purify the sons of Levi and refine them like gold and silver, and they will bring offerings in righteousness to the LORD." (Mal 3:2-3)

It is also important for the people or church to identify corporate sins like found in Daniel 9, Ezra 9, Nehemiah 9. Corporate sins may include the following among others;

- Church split
- Adopting the ways of the world
- Fighting church leaders unjustly
- Doing good instead of best
- Envy, jealousy, controversy
- Covering up sin
- Defaulting debt and refusing to pay
- Disgracing God's name by moral failures
- Failing to care for the needs of the vulnerable
- Failing to take strong stand on God's standards for family and marriage
- Disunity
- Lack of faith to attempt God sized ventures
- Leaving a ministry field for comfort zones
- Discrimination and nepotism or racism
- Refusing church discipline
- Refusing to obey god on ventures that are costly on your life
- Usurping Christ's authority over the church
- Tolerating evil in the congregations
- Collaborating with rights movements that are promoting sinister activities
- Selfishly using resources for personal comforts instead of the needy ETC

Prepare your heart, life and obey the call of God on your life and you will see the hand of the Lord on your life, family, church and nation. You are the hope for your generation to see God in your life. Fear not for the Lord will defend those who stand courageously in this course.

www.ingramcontent.com/pod-product-compliance
Lightning Source LLC
Chambersburg PA
CBHW020536160726
47992CB00012B/2459